GRAPHIC LIBRARY

D0557353

GRAPHIC BIOGRAPHIES

BESSIE COLEMAN
DARING STUNT PILOT

by Trina Robbins
illustrated by Ken Steacy

Consultant:
Margie Richison
Chairman, Board of Trustees
Museum of Women Pilots
Oklahoma City, Oklahoma

Capstone
press

Mankato, Minnesota

Graphic Library is published by Capstone Press,
1710 Roe Crest Drive, North Mankato, Minnesota 56003.
www.capstonepress.com

Copyright © 2007 by Capstone Press. All rights reserved.
No part of this publication may be reproduced in whole or in part, or stored in a
retrieval system, or transmitted in any form or by any means, electronic, mechanical,
photocopying, recording, or otherwise, without written permission of the publisher.
For information regarding permission, write to Capstone Press,
1710 Roe Crest Drive, North Mankato, Minnesota 56003.

Printed in the United States of America.
072019   002451

Library of Congress Cataloging-in-Publication Data
Robbins, Trina.
    Bessie Coleman : daring stunt pilot / by Trina Robbins ; Illustrated by Ken Steacy.
    p. cm.—(Graphic library. Graphic biographies)
    Summary: "In graphic novel format, tells the story of Bessie Coleman, the daring stunt pilot"
Provided by publisher.
    Includes bibliographical references and index.
    ISBN-13: 978-0-7368-6851-8 (hard cover)
    ISBN-10: 0-7368-6851-8 (hard cover)
    ISBN-13: 978-0-7368-7903-3 (softcover pbk.)
    ISBN-10: 0-7368-7903-X (softcover pbk.)
    1. Coleman, Bessie, 1896–1926—Juvenile literature. 2. Air pilots—United States—
Biography—Juvenile literature. 3. African American women air pilots—Biography—Juvenile
literature. I. Title. II. Series.
TL540.C646R63 2007
629.13092—dc22
[B]   2006026615

Designer
Jason Knudson

Editor
Rebecca Glaser

Editor's note: Direct quotations from primary sources are indicated by a yellow background.

Direct quotations appear on the following pages:
Page 4, from *Memoirs of the Late Bessie Coleman* by Elois Coleman Patterson, quoted in
    Bessie Coleman: The Brownskin Ladybird by Elizabeth Hadley Freydberg (New York:
    Garland Publishing, 1994).
Page 13, from interviews with Marion Coleman; page 23, telegram, both quoted in *Queen Bess:
    Daredevil Aviator* by Doris L. Rich (Washington, D.C.: Smithsonian Institution Press,
    1993).
Pages 19 (both), 24 (left), "Aviatrix Must Sign Away Life to Learn Trade," *Chicago Defender,*
    October 8, 1921.
Page 21, ad for Coleman's barnstorming show, *Chicago Defender*, October 14, 1922, reprinted
    in *Bessie Coleman: The Brownskin Ladybird* by Elizabeth Hadley Freydberg (New York:
    Garland Publishing, 1994).
Page 24, "Color Bar Forces Woman to Go to France," June 1, 1921, reprinted in *Women Aloft*
    by Valerie Moolman (Alexandria, VA: Time-Life Books, 1981).

TABLE OF CONTENTS

Chapter 1
Dirt Poor in Texas. 4

Chapter 2
Chicago 10

Chapter 3
Flight School in France 16

Chapter 4
The Sky's No Limit 20

More about Bessie Coleman 28
Glossary 30
Internet Sites 30
Read More. 31
Bibliography. 31
Index 32

Chapter 1
Dirt Poor in Texas

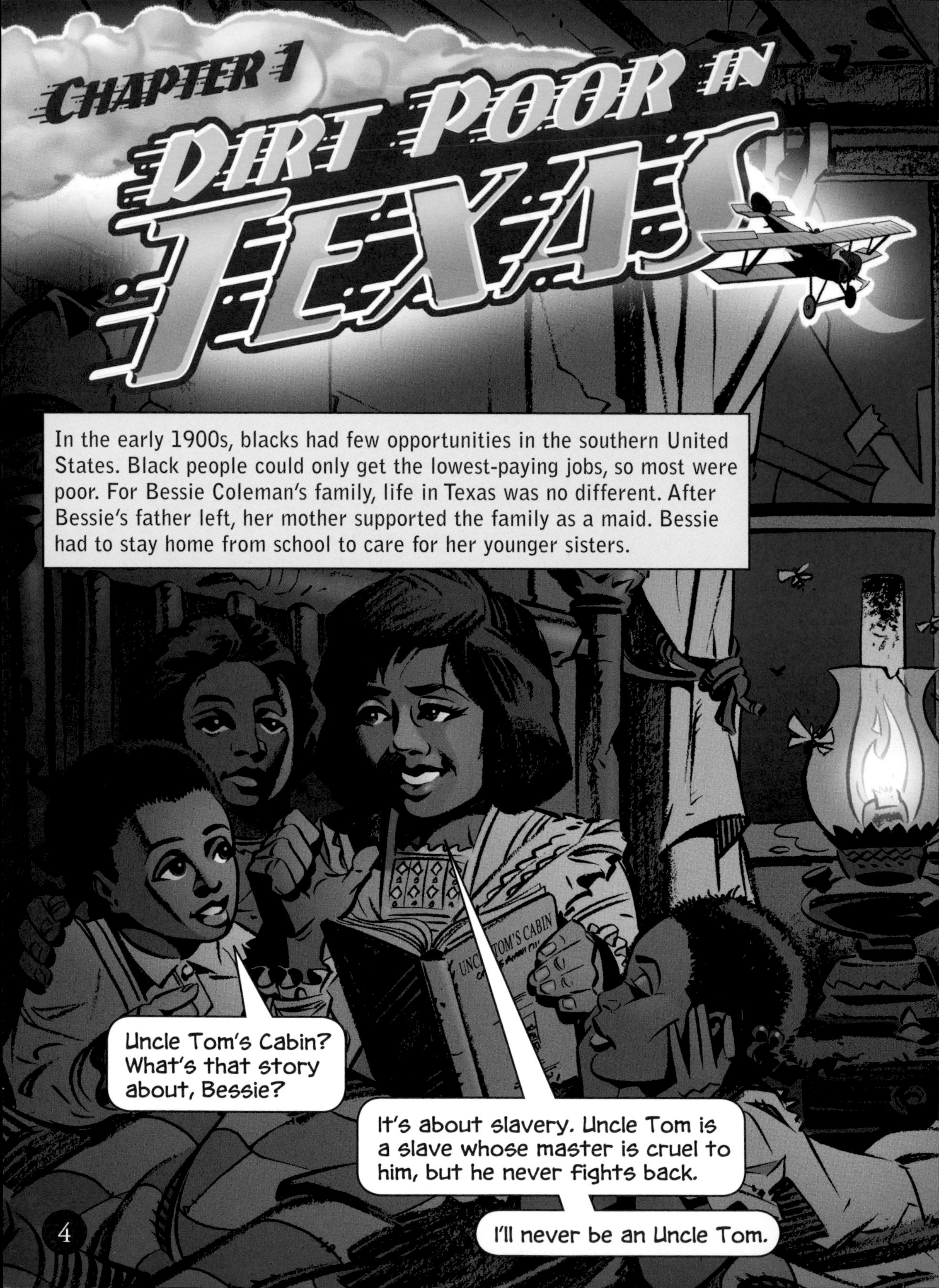
In the early 1900s, blacks had few opportunities in the southern United States. Black people could only get the lowest-paying jobs, so most were poor. For Bessie Coleman's family, life in Texas was no different. After Bessie's father left, her mother supported the family as a maid. Bessie had to stay home from school to care for her younger sisters.
Uncle Tom's Cabin? What's that story about, Bessie?
It's about slavery. Uncle Tom is a slave whose master is cruel to him, but he never fights back.
I'll never be an Uncle Tom.

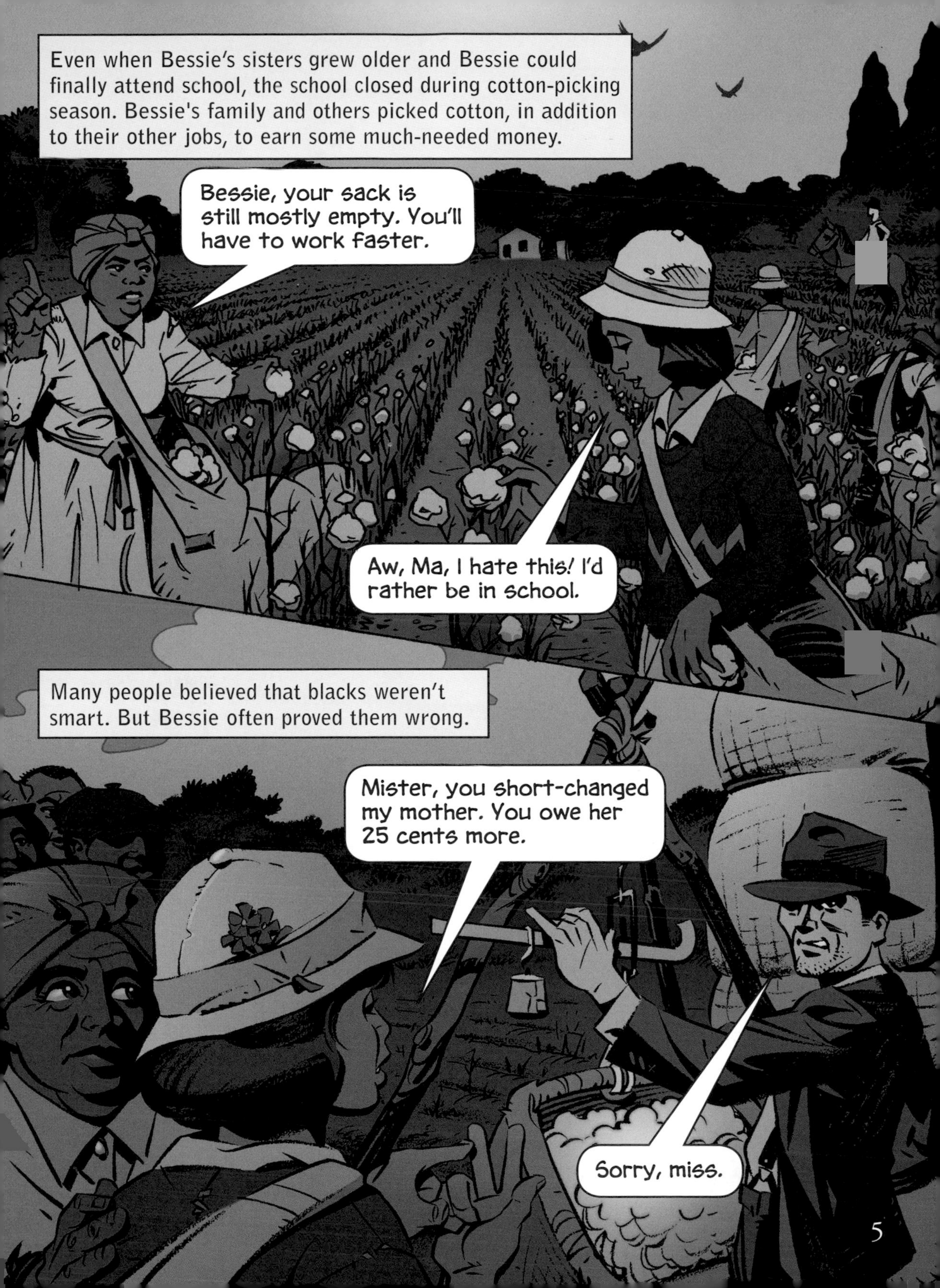
Even when Bessie's sisters grew older and Bessie could finally attend school, the school closed during cotton-picking season. Bessie's family and others picked cotton, in addition to their other jobs, to earn some much-needed money.
Bessie, your sack is still mostly empty. You'll have to work faster.
Aw, Ma, I hate this! I'd rather be in school.
Many people believed that blacks weren't smart. But Bessie often proved them wrong.
Mister, you short-changed my mother. You owe her 25 cents more.
Sorry, miss.

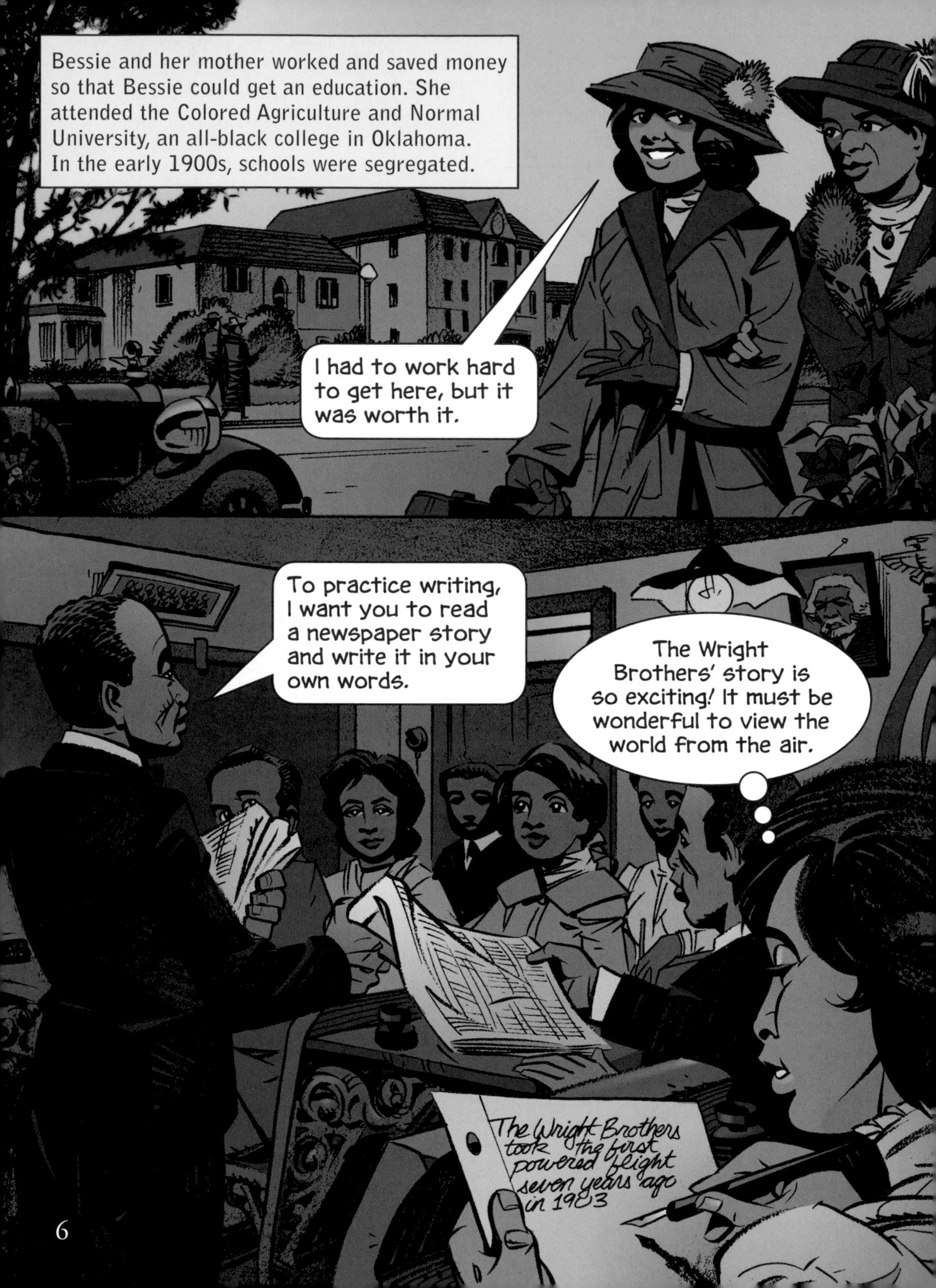
Bessie and her mother worked and saved money so that Bessie could get an education. She attended the Colored Agriculture and Normal University, an all-black college in Oklahoma. In the early 1900s, schools were segregated.
I had to work hard to get here, but it was worth it.
To practice writing, I want you to read a newspaper story and write it in your own words.
The Wright Brothers' story is so exciting! It must be wonderful to view the world from the air.
The Wright Brothers took the first powered flight seven years ago in 1903

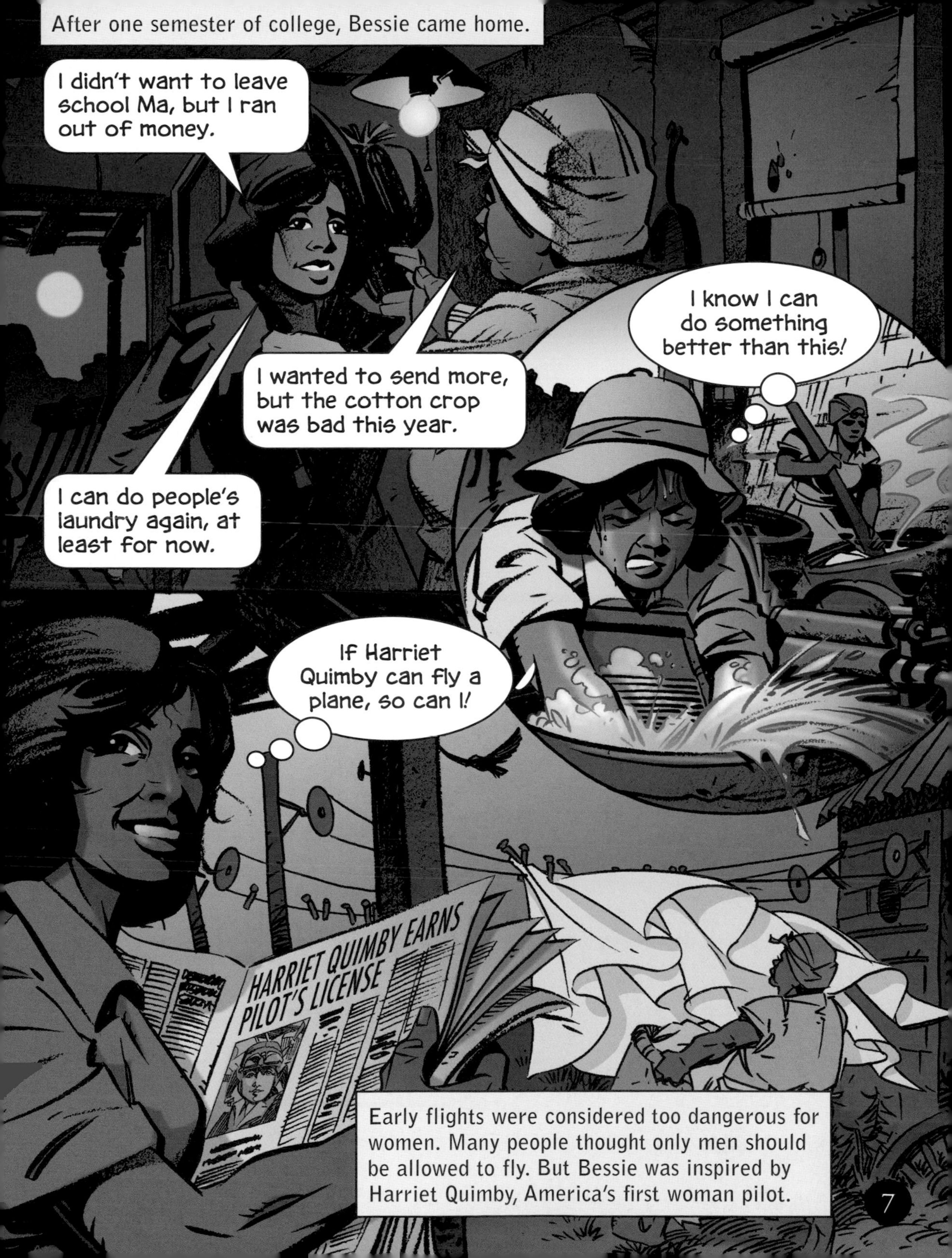
After one semester of college, Bessie came home.
I didn't want to leave school Ma, but I ran out of money.
I wanted to send more, but the cotton crop was bad this year.
I can do people's laundry again, at least for now.
I know I can do something better than this!
If Harriet Quimby can fly a plane, so can I!
HARRIET QUIMBY EARNS PILOT'S LICENSE
Early flights were considered too dangerous for women. Many people thought only men should be allowed to fly. But Bessie was inspired by Harriet Quimby, America's first woman pilot.

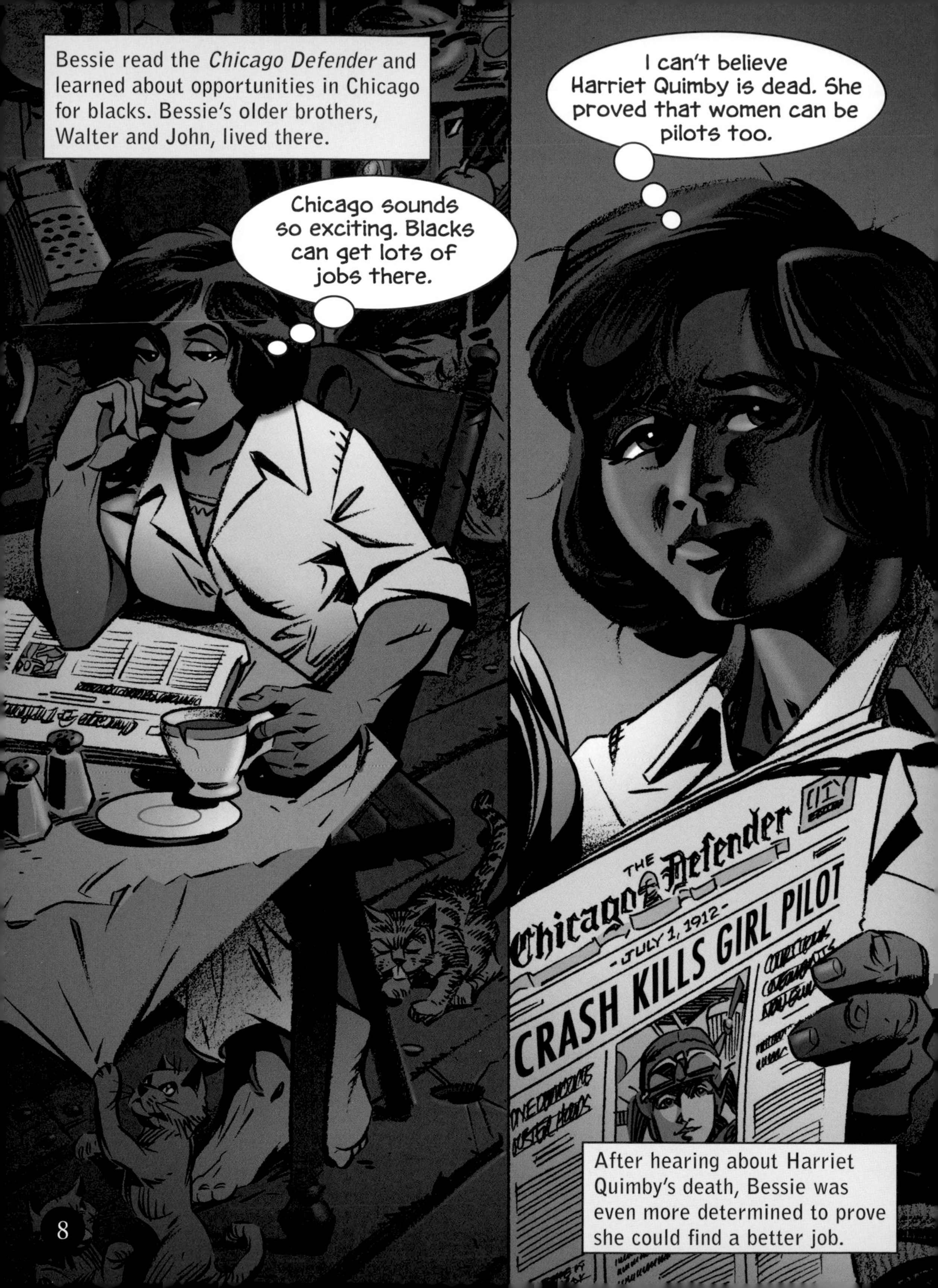
Bessie read the *Chicago Defender* and learned about opportunities in Chicago for blacks. Bessie's older brothers, Walter and John, lived there.
Chicago sounds so exciting. Blacks can get lots of jobs there.
I can't believe Harriet Quimby is dead. She proved that women can be pilots too.
THE Chicago Defender
JULY 1, 1912
CRASH KILLS GIRL PILOT
After hearing about Harriet Quimby's death, Bessie was even more determined to prove she could find a better job.

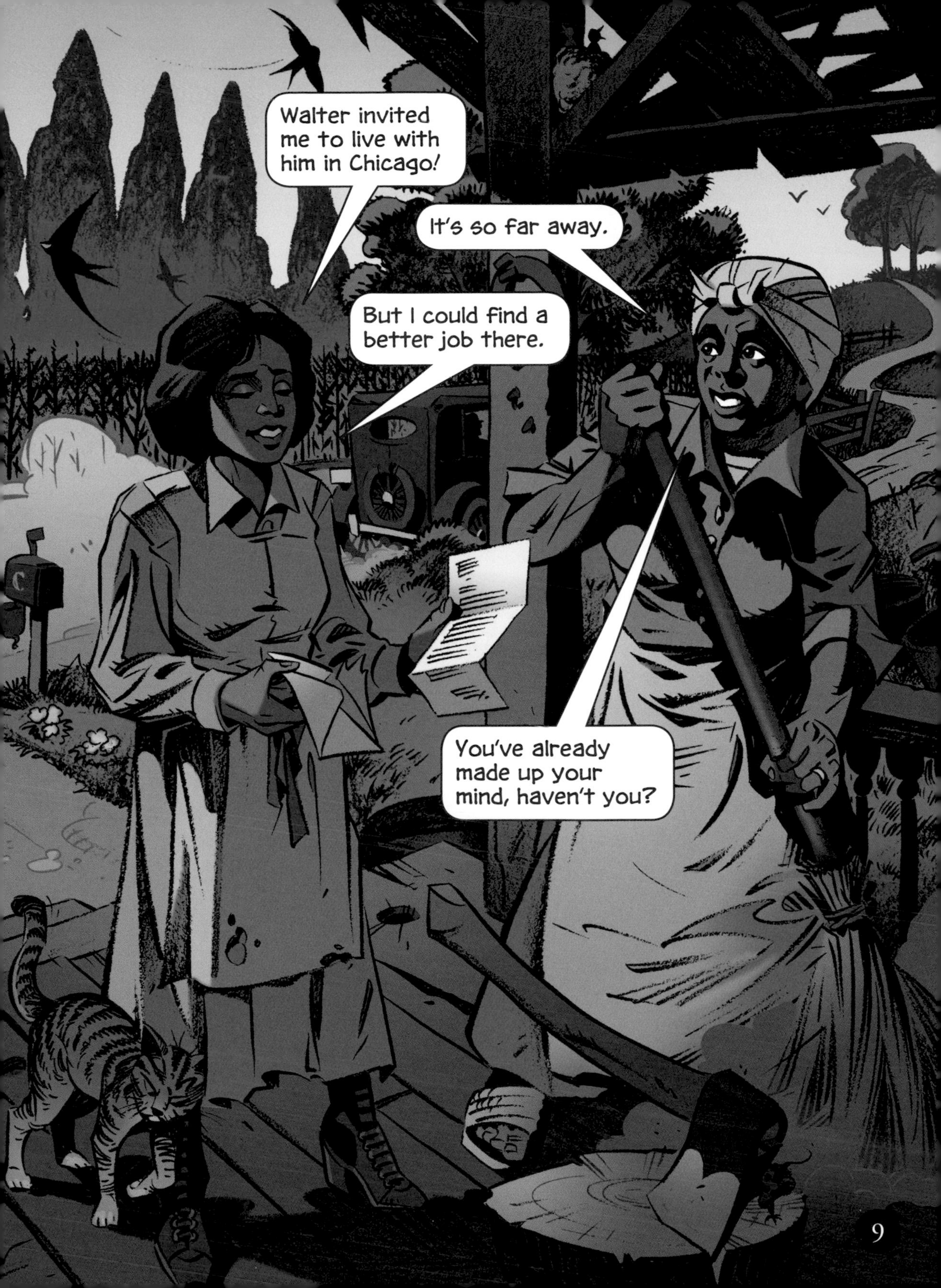
Walter invited me to live with him in Chicago!
It's so far away.
But I could find a better job there.
You've already made up your mind, haven't you?

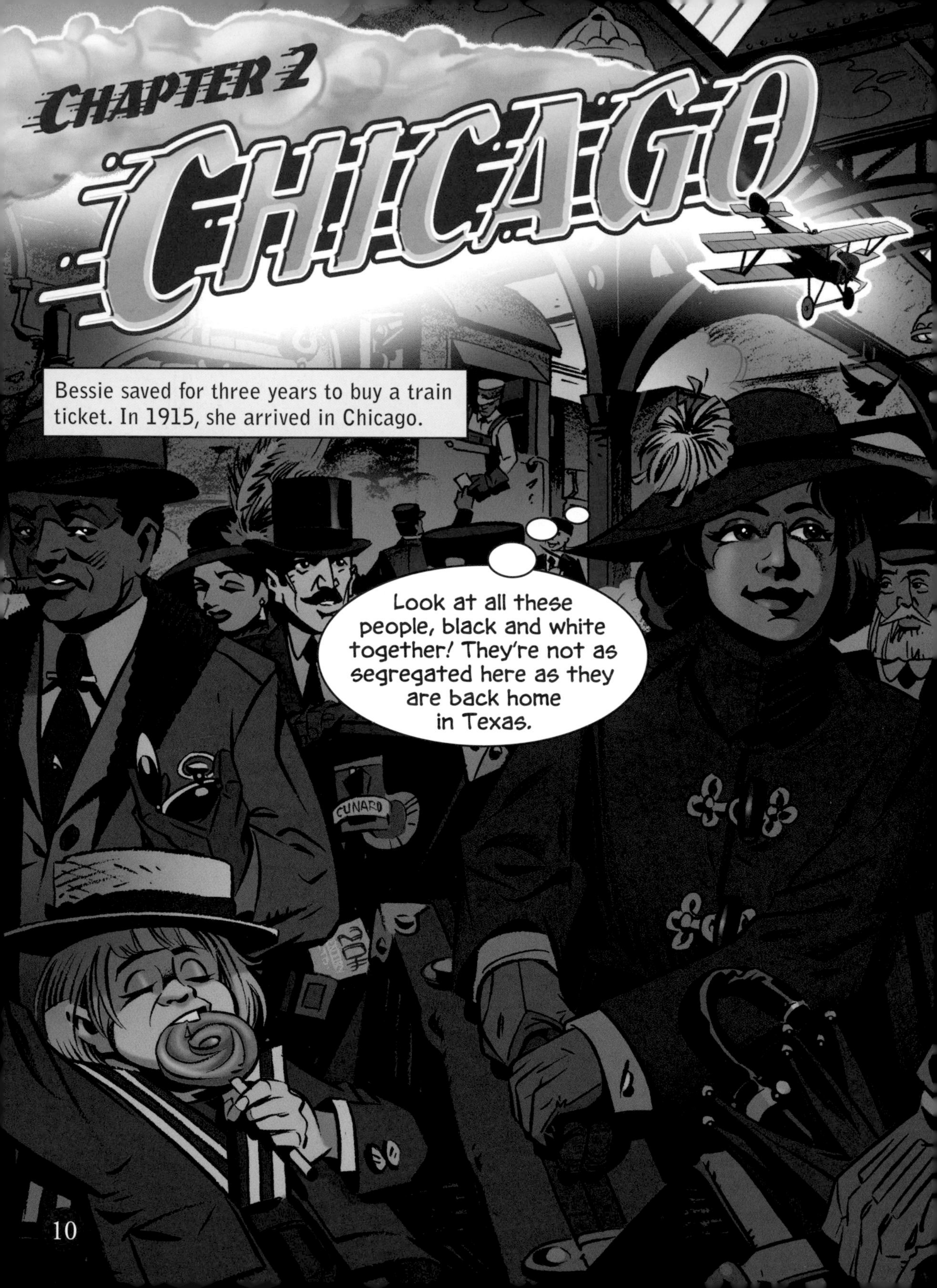
CHAPTER 2
CHICAGO
Bessie saved for three years to buy a train ticket. In 1915, she arrived in Chicago.
Look at all these people, black and white together! They're not as segregated here as they are back home in Texas.
CUNARD

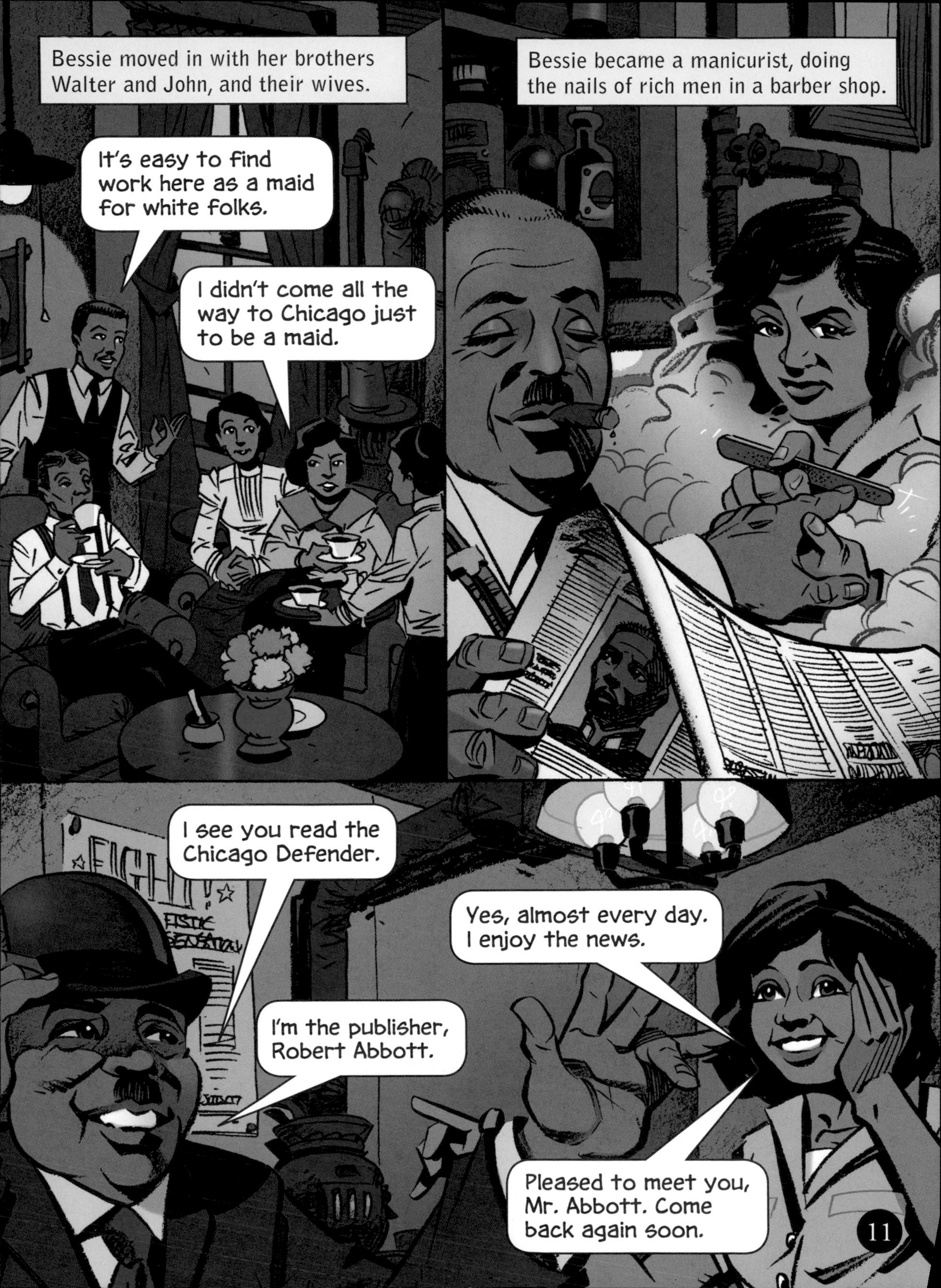
Bessie moved in with her brothers Walter and John, and their wives.
It's easy to find work here as a maid for white folks.
I didn't come all the way to Chicago just to be a maid.
Bessie became a manicurist, doing the nails of rich men in a barber shop.
I see you read the Chicago Defender.
I'm the publisher, Robert Abbott.
Yes, almost every day. I enjoy the news.
Pleased to meet you, Mr. Abbott. Come back again soon.

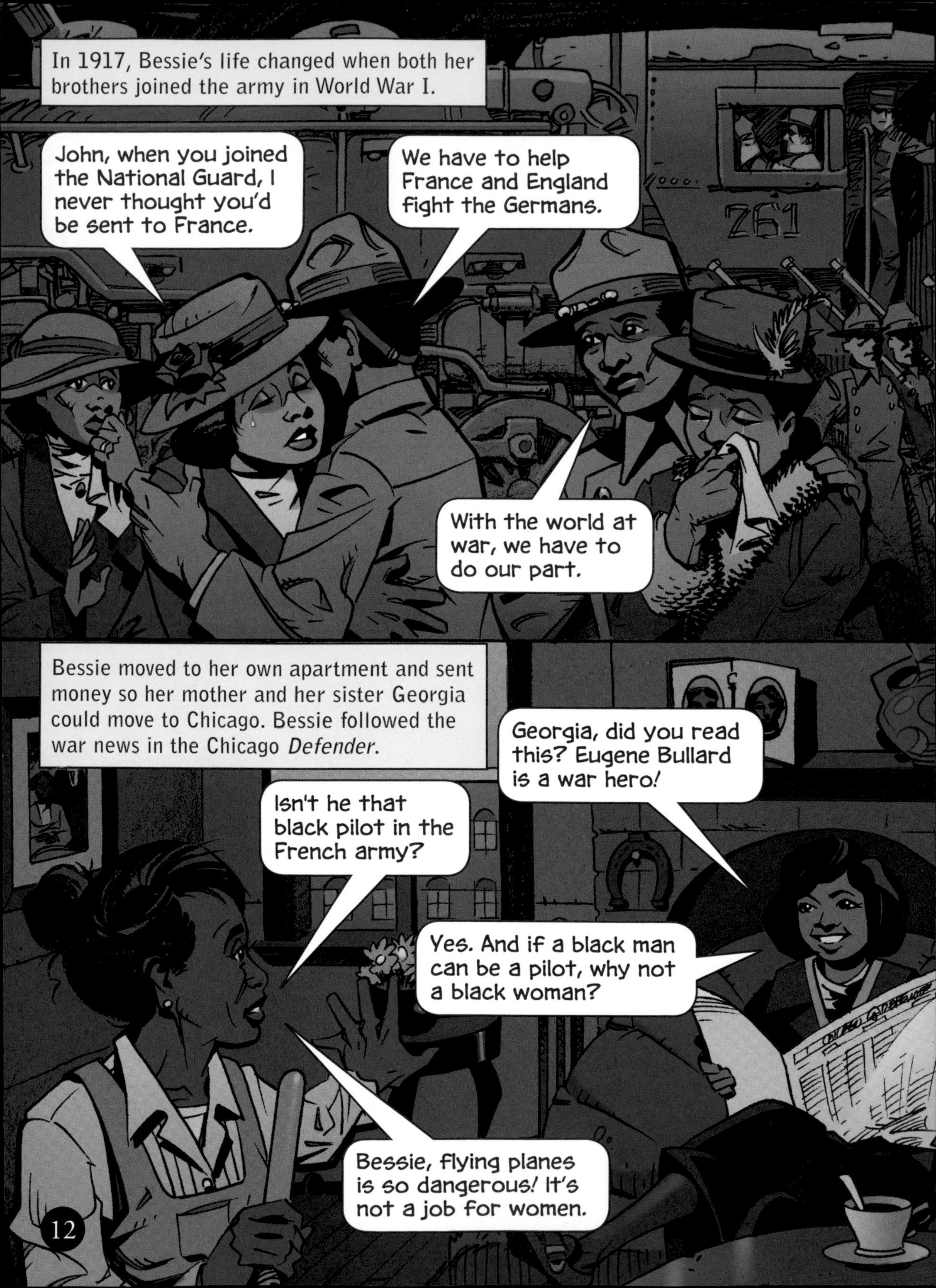
In 1917, Bessie's life changed when both her brothers joined the army in World War I.
John, when you joined the National Guard, I never thought you'd be sent to France.
We have to help France and England fight the Germans.
With the world at war, we have to do our part.
Bessie moved to her own apartment and sent money so her mother and her sister Georgia could move to Chicago. Bessie followed the war news in the Chicago *Defender*.
Georgia, did you read this? Eugene Bullard is a war hero!
Isn't he that black pilot in the French army?
Yes. And if a black man can be a pilot, why not a black woman?
Bessie, flying planes is so dangerous! It's not a job for women.

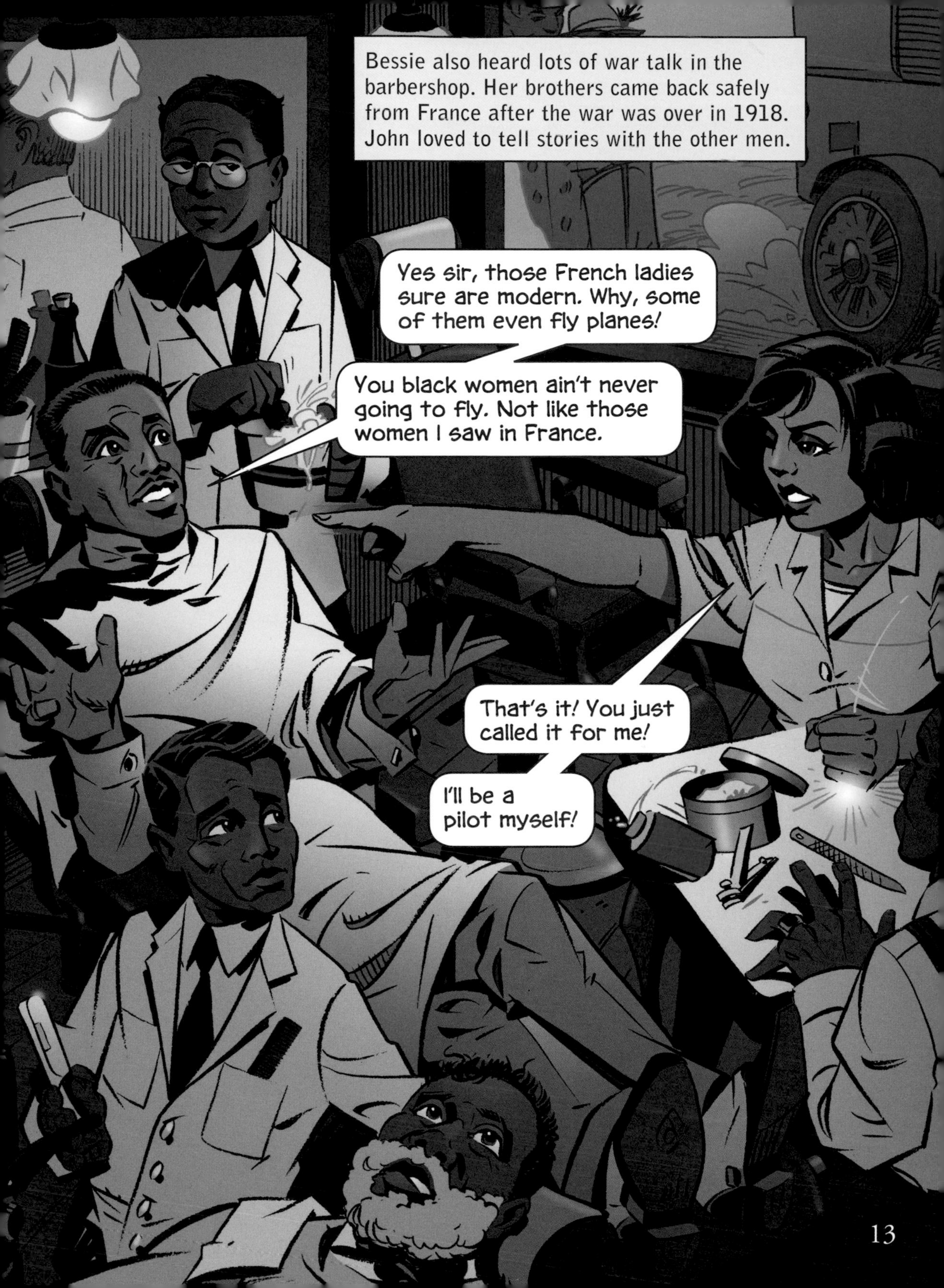

Bessie also heard lots of war talk in the barbershop. Her brothers came back safely from France after the war was over in 1918. John loved to tell stories with the other men.
Yes sir, those French ladies sure are modern. Why, some of them even fly planes!
You black women ain't never going to fly. Not like those women I saw in France.
That's it! You just called it for me!
I'll be a pilot myself!

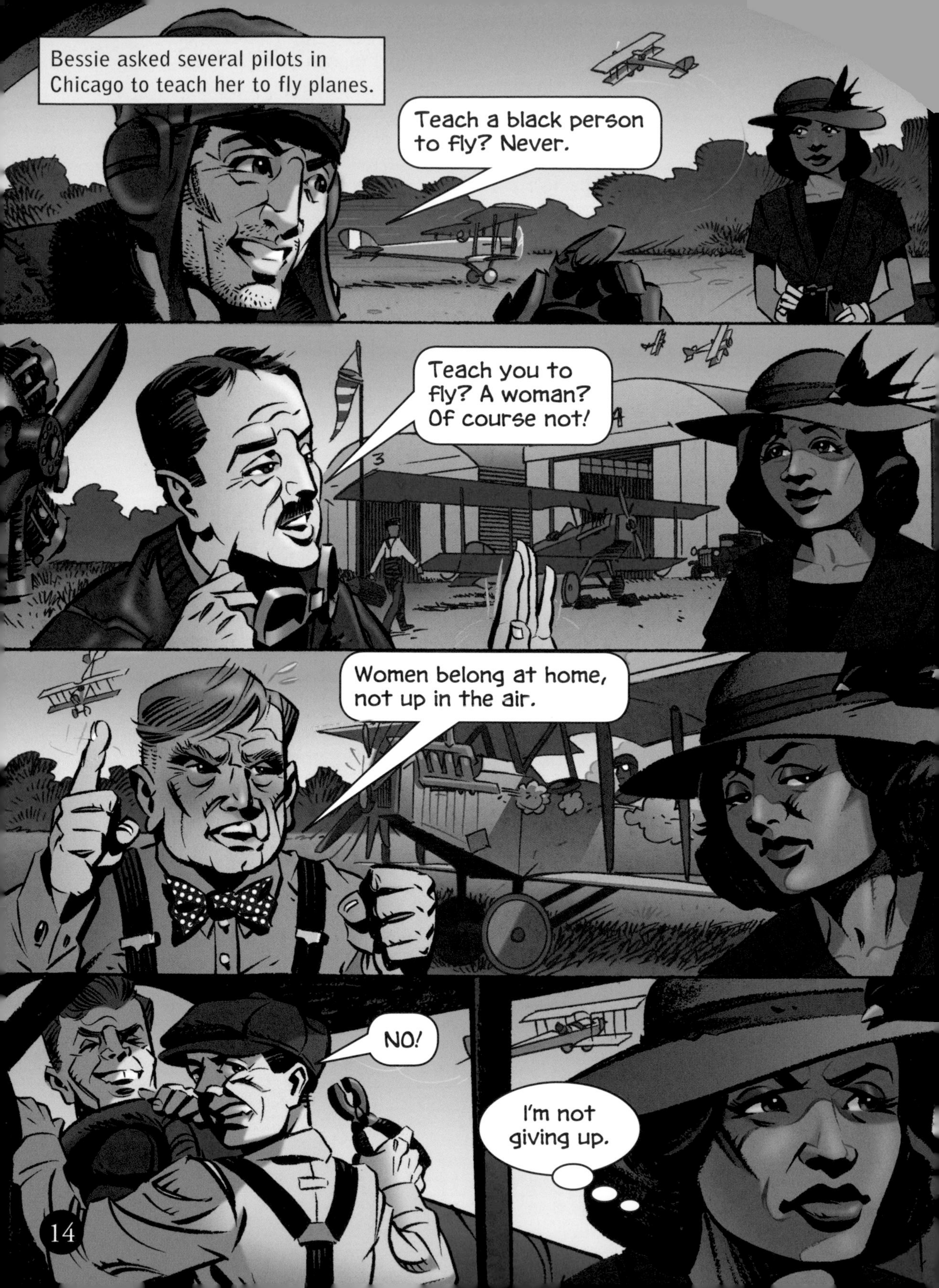
Bessie asked several pilots in Chicago to teach her to fly planes.
Teach a black person to fly? Never.
Teach you to fly? A woman? Of course not!
Women belong at home, not up in the air.
NO!
I'm not giving up.

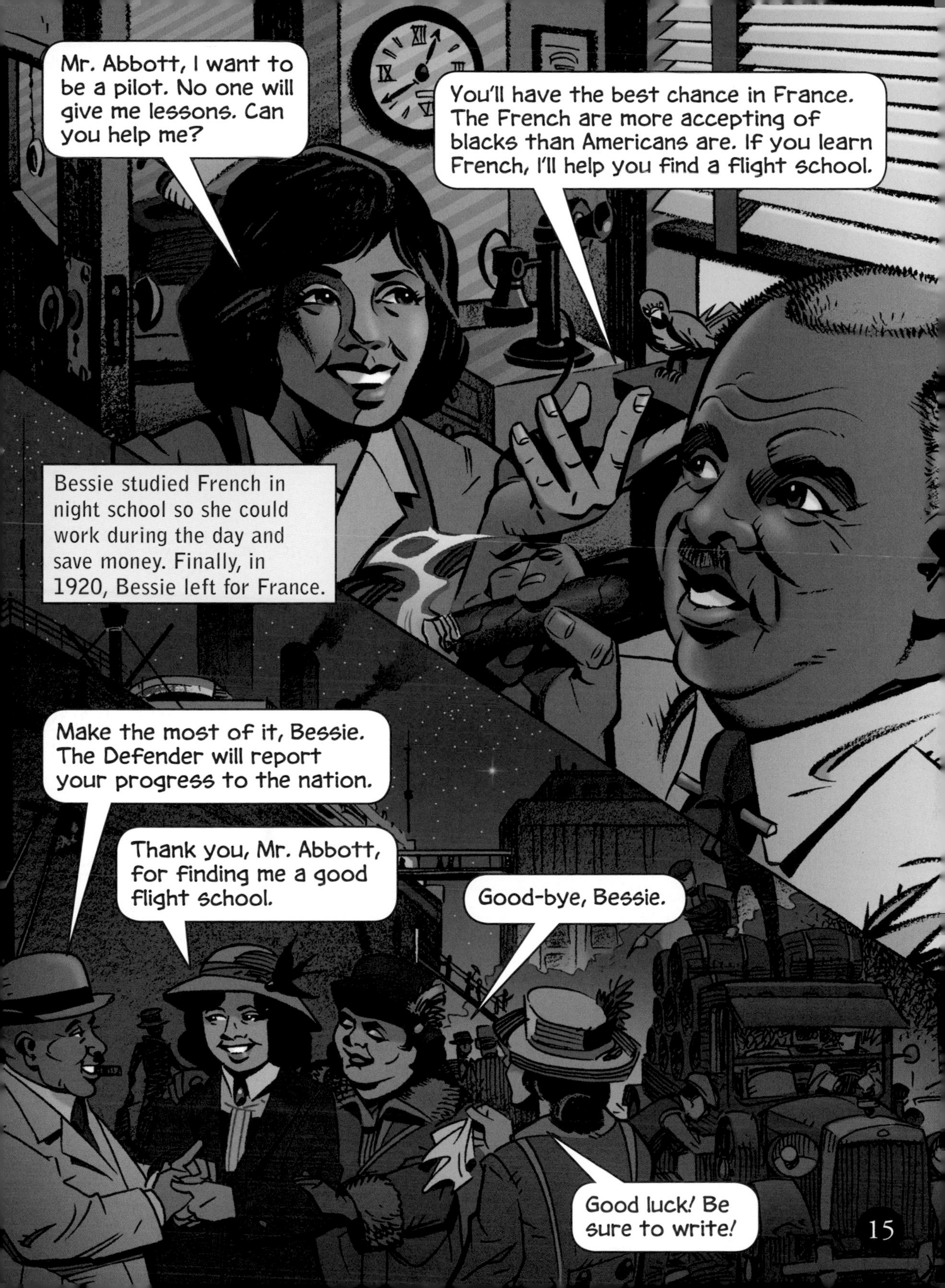
Mr. Abbott, I want to be a pilot. No one will give me lessons. Can you help me?
You'll have the best chance in France. The French are more accepting of blacks than Americans are. If you learn French, I'll help you find a flight school.
Bessie studied French in night school so she could work during the day and save money. Finally, in 1920, Bessie left for France.
Make the most of it, Bessie. The Defender will report your progress to the nation.
Thank you, Mr. Abbott, for finding me a good flight school.
Good-bye, Bessie.
Good luck! Be sure to write!

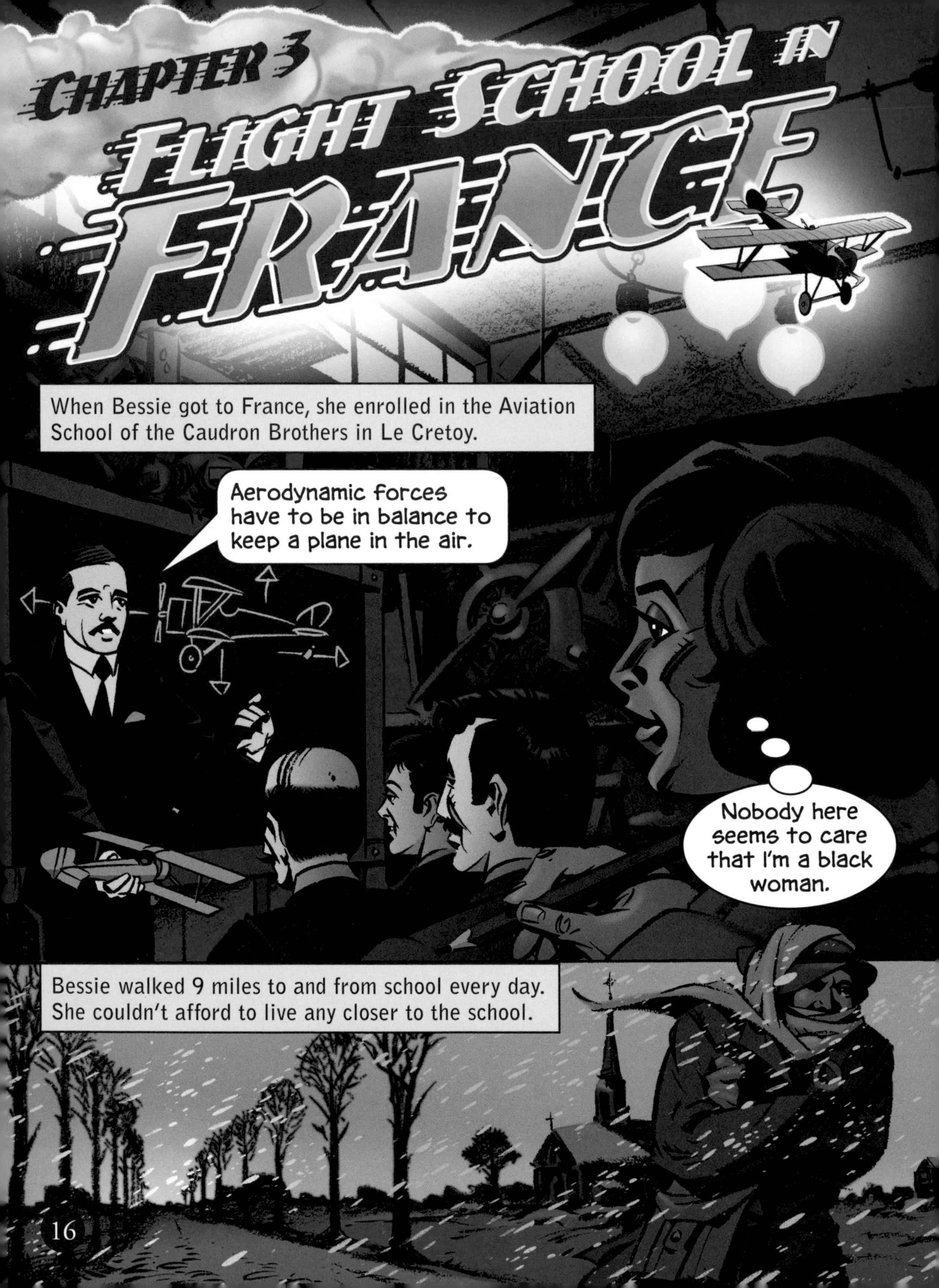
CHAPTER 3
FLIGHT SCHOOL IN FRANCE
When Bessie got to France, she enrolled in the Aviation School of the Caudron Brothers in Le Cretoy.
Aerodynamic forces have to be in balance to keep a plane in the air.
Nobody here seems to care that I'm a black woman.
Bessie walked 9 miles to and from school every day. She couldn't afford to live any closer to the school.

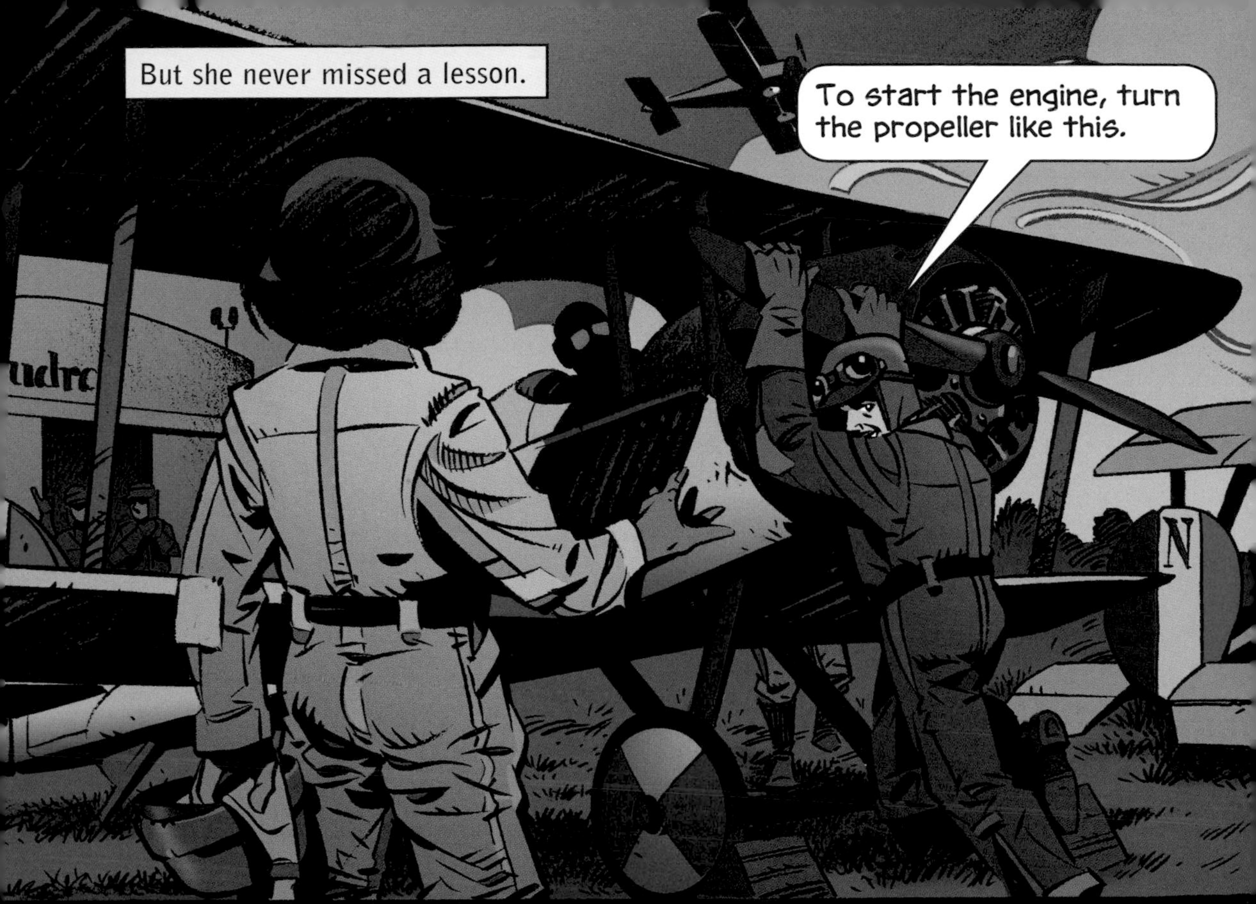
But she never missed a lesson.
To start the engine, turn the propeller like this.

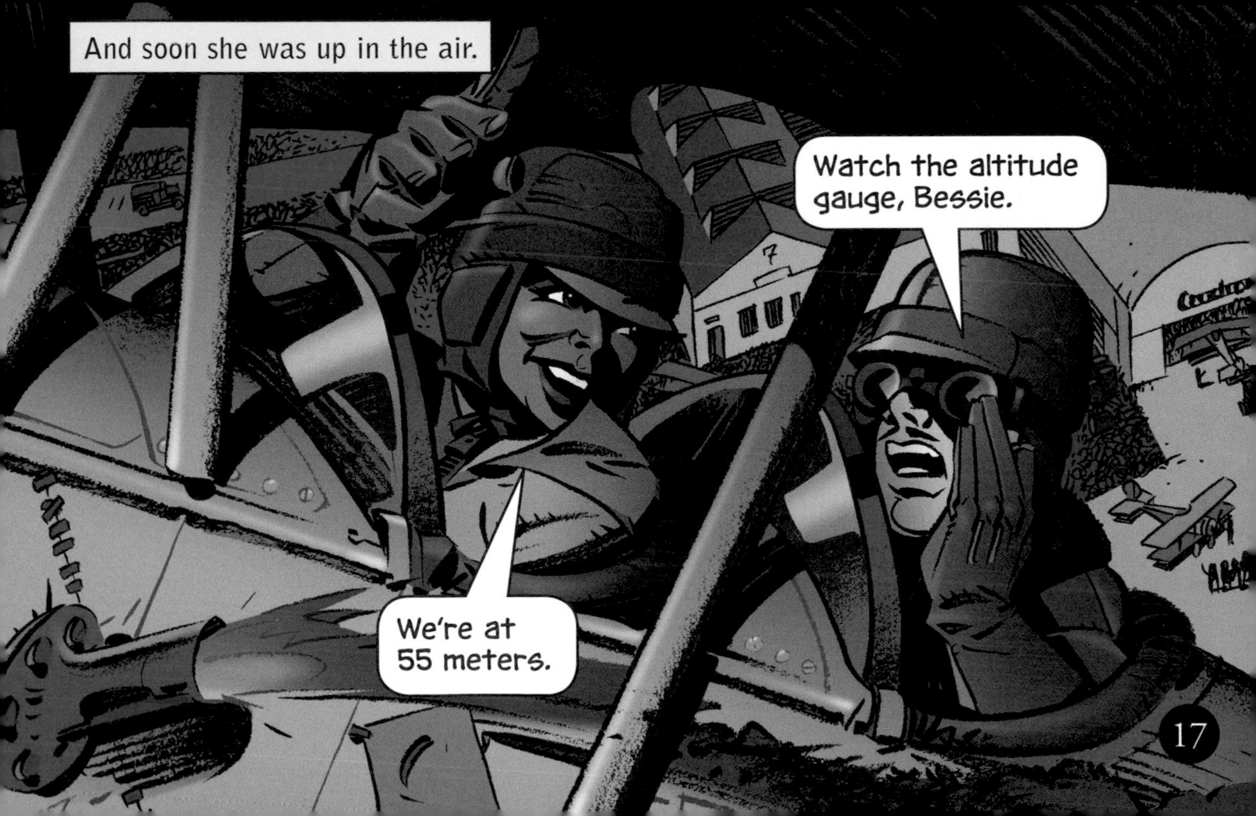
And soon she was up in the air.
Watch the altitude gauge, Bessie.
We're at 55 meters.

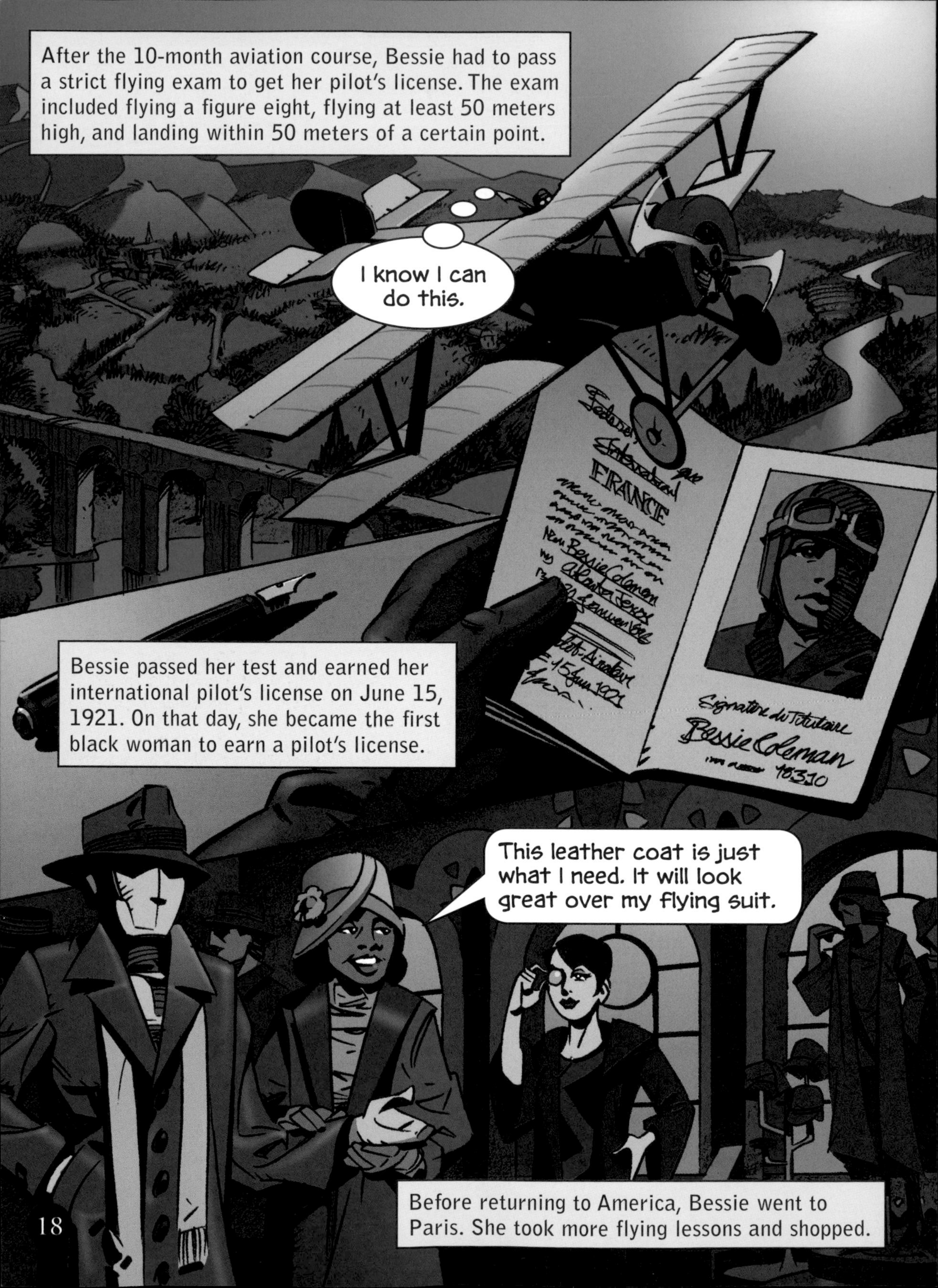
After the 10-month aviation course, Bessie had to pass a strict flying exam to get her pilot's license. The exam included flying a figure eight, flying at least 50 meters high, and landing within 50 meters of a certain point.
I know I can do this.
FRANCE
Bessie Coleman
Bessie passed her test and earned her international pilot's license on June 15, 1921. On that day, she became the first black woman to earn a pilot's license.
This leather coat is just what I need. It will look great over my flying suit.
Before returning to America, Bessie went to Paris. She took more flying lessons and shopped.

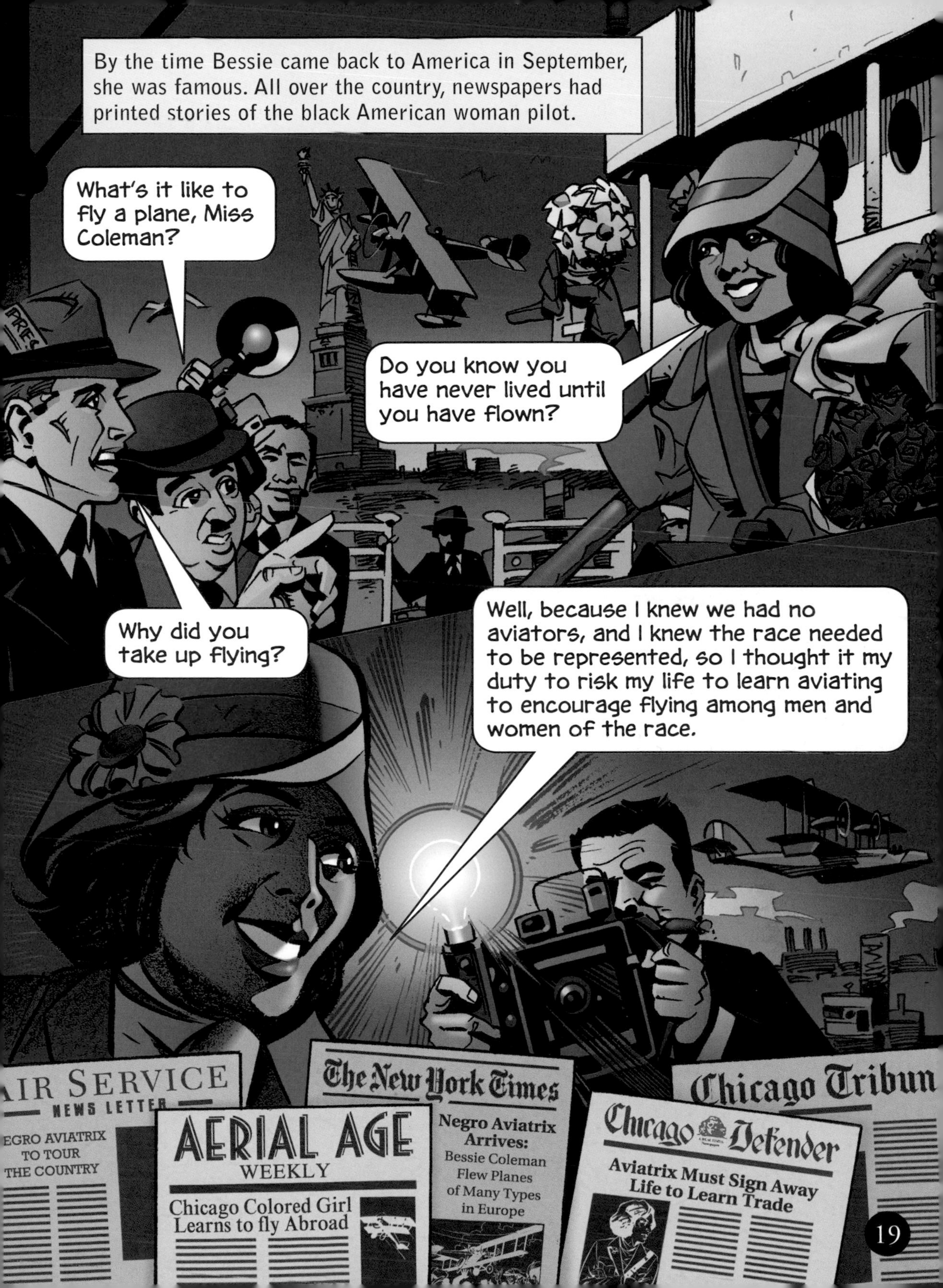
By the time Bessie came back to America in September, she was famous. All over the country, newspapers had printed stories of the black American woman pilot.
What's it like to fly a plane, Miss Coleman?
Do you know you have never lived until you have flown?
Why did you take up flying?
Well, because I knew we had no aviators, and I knew the race needed to be represented, so I thought it my duty to risk my life to learn aviating to encourage flying among men and women of the race.
IR SERVICE
NEWS LETTE
EGRO AVIATRIX TO TOUR THE COUNTRY
AERIAL AGE WEEKLY
Chicago Colored Girl Learns to fly Abroad
The New York Times
Negro Aviatrix Arrives: Bessie Coleman Flew Planes of Many Types in Europe
Chicago Tribun
Chicago Defender
Aviatrix Must Sign Away Life to Learn Trade

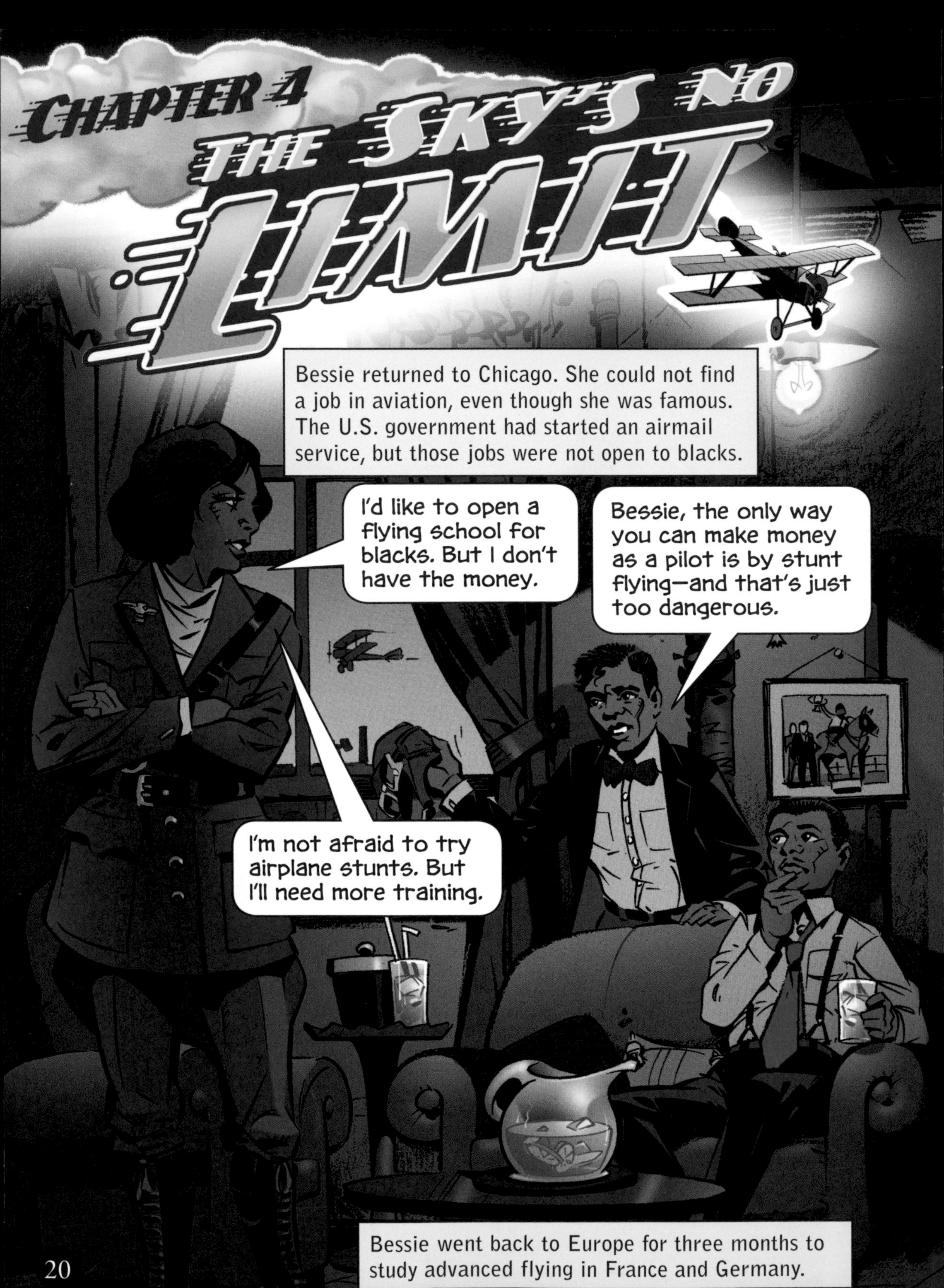
CHAPTER 4
THE SKY'S NO LIMIT
Bessie returned to Chicago. She could not find a job in aviation, even though she was famous. The U.S. government had started an airmail service, but those jobs were not open to blacks.
I'd like to open a flying school for blacks. But I don't have the money.
Bessie, the only way you can make money as a pilot is by stunt flying—and that's just too dangerous.
I'm not afraid to try airplane stunts. But I'll need more training.
Bessie went back to Europe for three months to study advanced flying in France and Germany.

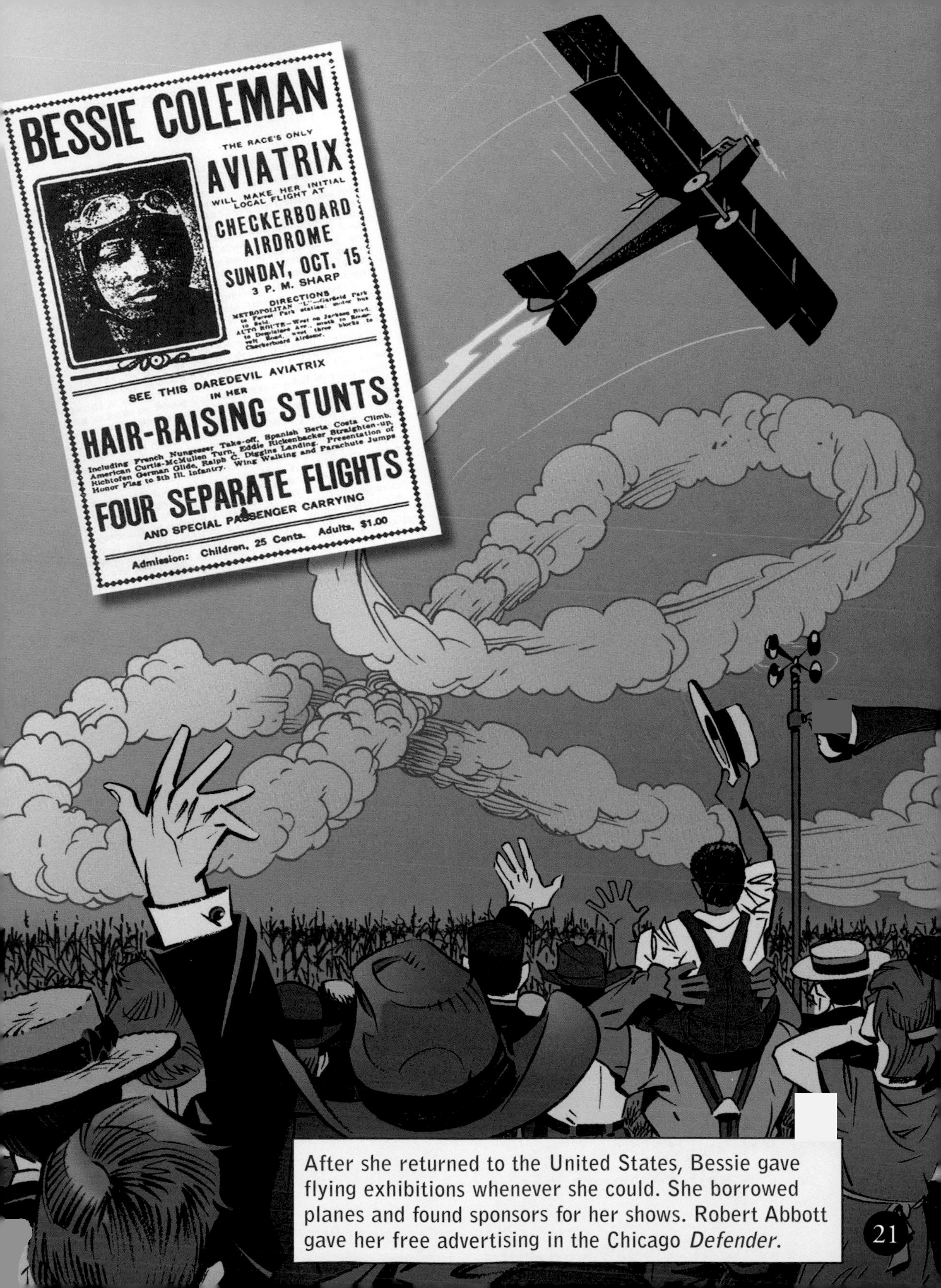
BESSIE COLEMAN
THE RACE'S ONLY
AVIATRIX
WILL MAKE HER INITIAL LOCAL FLIGHT AT
CHECKERBOARD AIRDROME
SUNDAY, OCT. 15
3 P. M. SHARP
DIRECTIONS
SEE THIS DAREDEVIL AVIATRIX IN HER
HAIR-RAISING STUNTS
Including French Nungesser Take-off, Spanish Berta Costa Climb, American Curtis-McMullen Turn, Eddie Rickenbacker Straighten-up, Richtofen German Glide, Ralph C. Diggins Landing. Presentation of Honor Flag to 8th Ill. Infantry. Wing Walking and Parachute Jumps
FOUR SEPARATE FLIGHTS
AND SPECIAL PASSENGER CARRYING
Admission: Children, 25 Cents. Adults, $1.00

After she returned to the United States, Bessie gave flying exhibitions whenever she could. She borrowed planes and found sponsors for her shows. Robert Abbott gave her free advertising in the Chicago *Defender*.

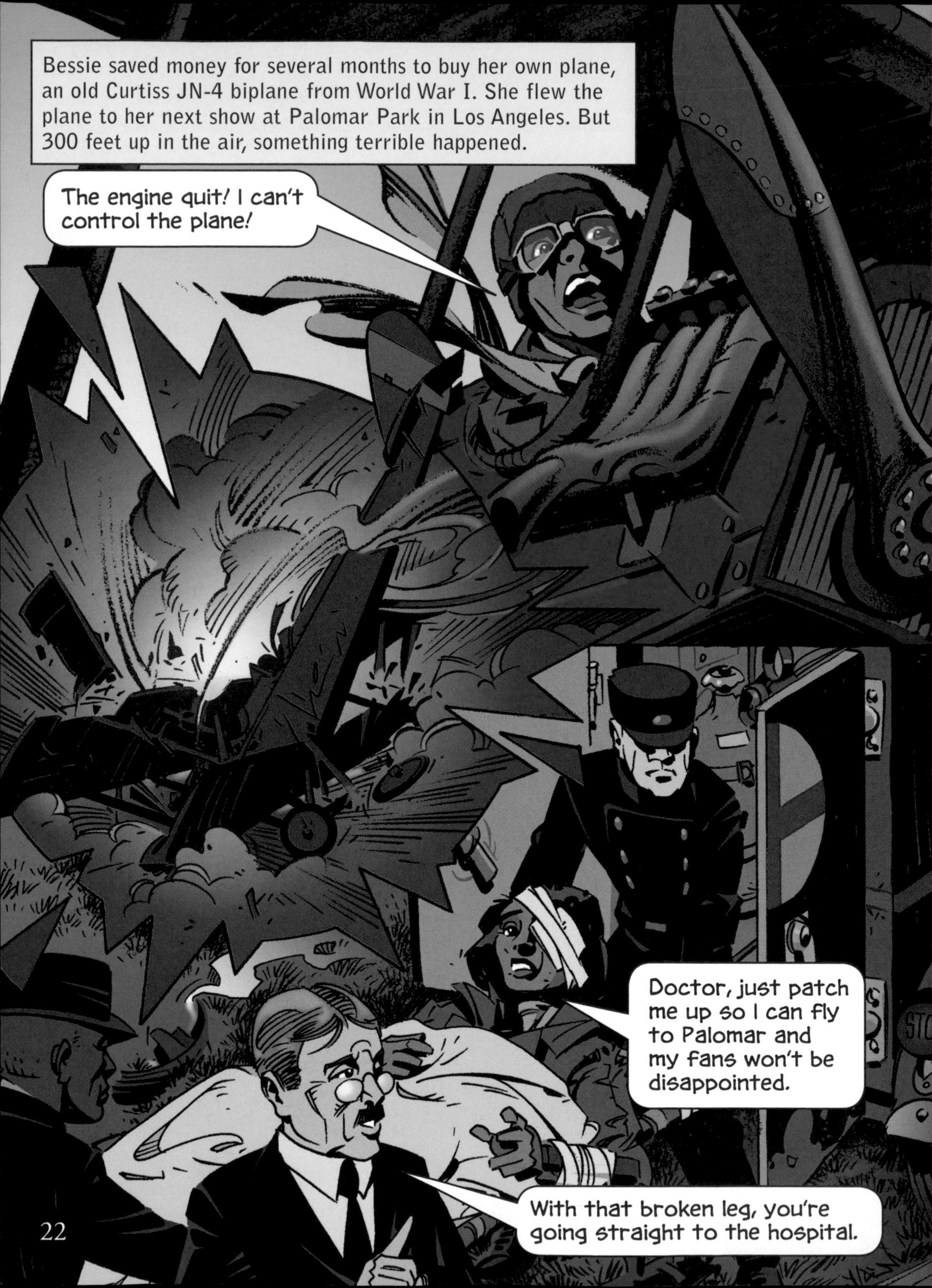
Bessie saved money for several months to buy her own plane, an old Curtiss JN-4 biplane from World War I. She flew the plane to her next show at Palomar Park in Los Angeles. But 300 feet up in the air, something terrible happened.
The engine quit! I can't control the plane!
Doctor, just patch me up so I can fly to Palomar and my fans won't be disappointed.
With that broken leg, you're going straight to the hospital.

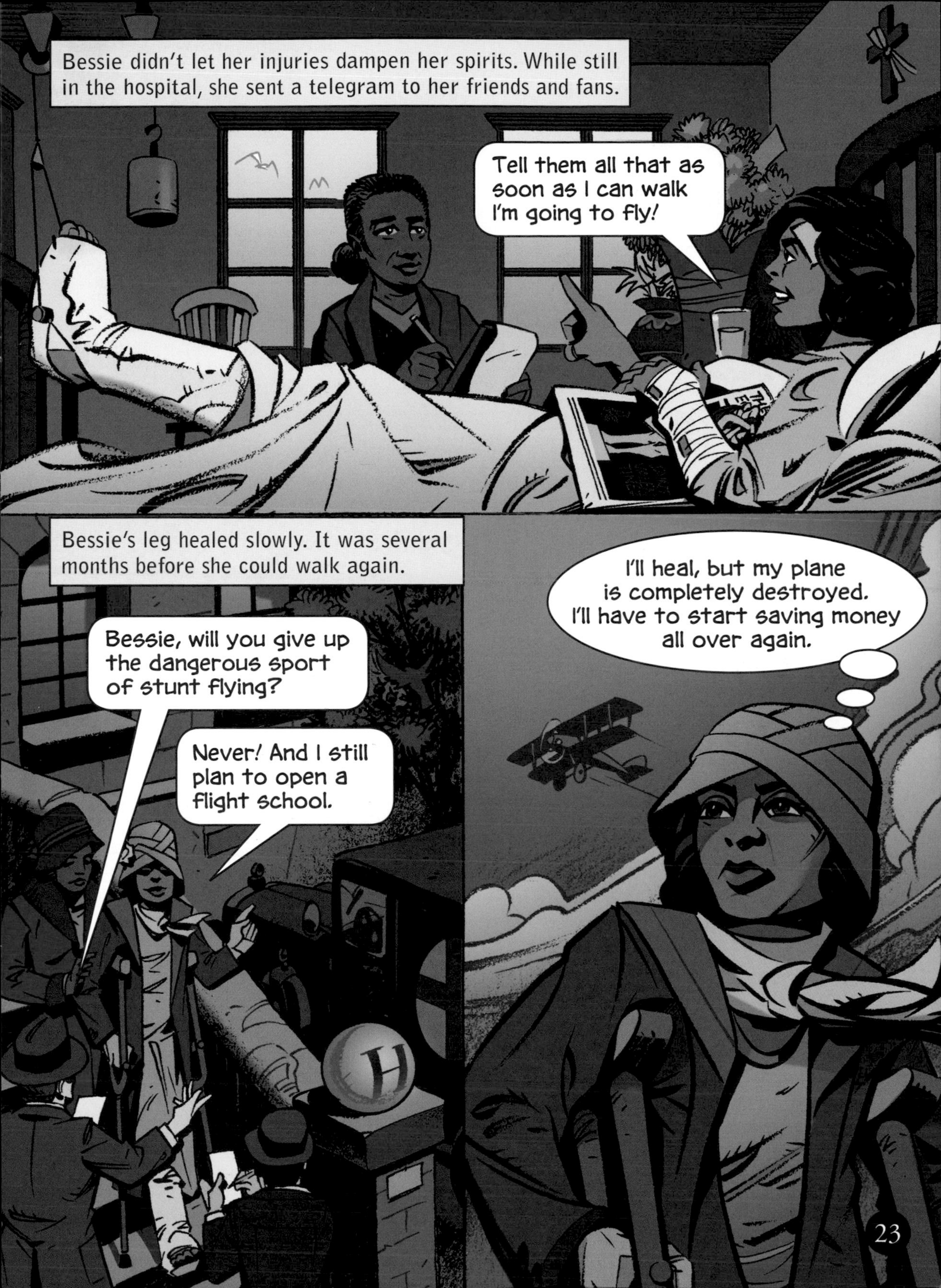

Bessie didn't let her injuries dampen her spirits. While still in the hospital, she sent a telegram to her friends and fans.
Tell them all that as soon as I can walk I'm going to fly!
Bessie's leg healed slowly. It was several months before she could walk again.
Bessie, will you give up the dangerous sport of stunt flying?
Never! And I still plan to open a flight school.
I'll heal, but my plane is completely destroyed. I'll have to start saving money all over again.

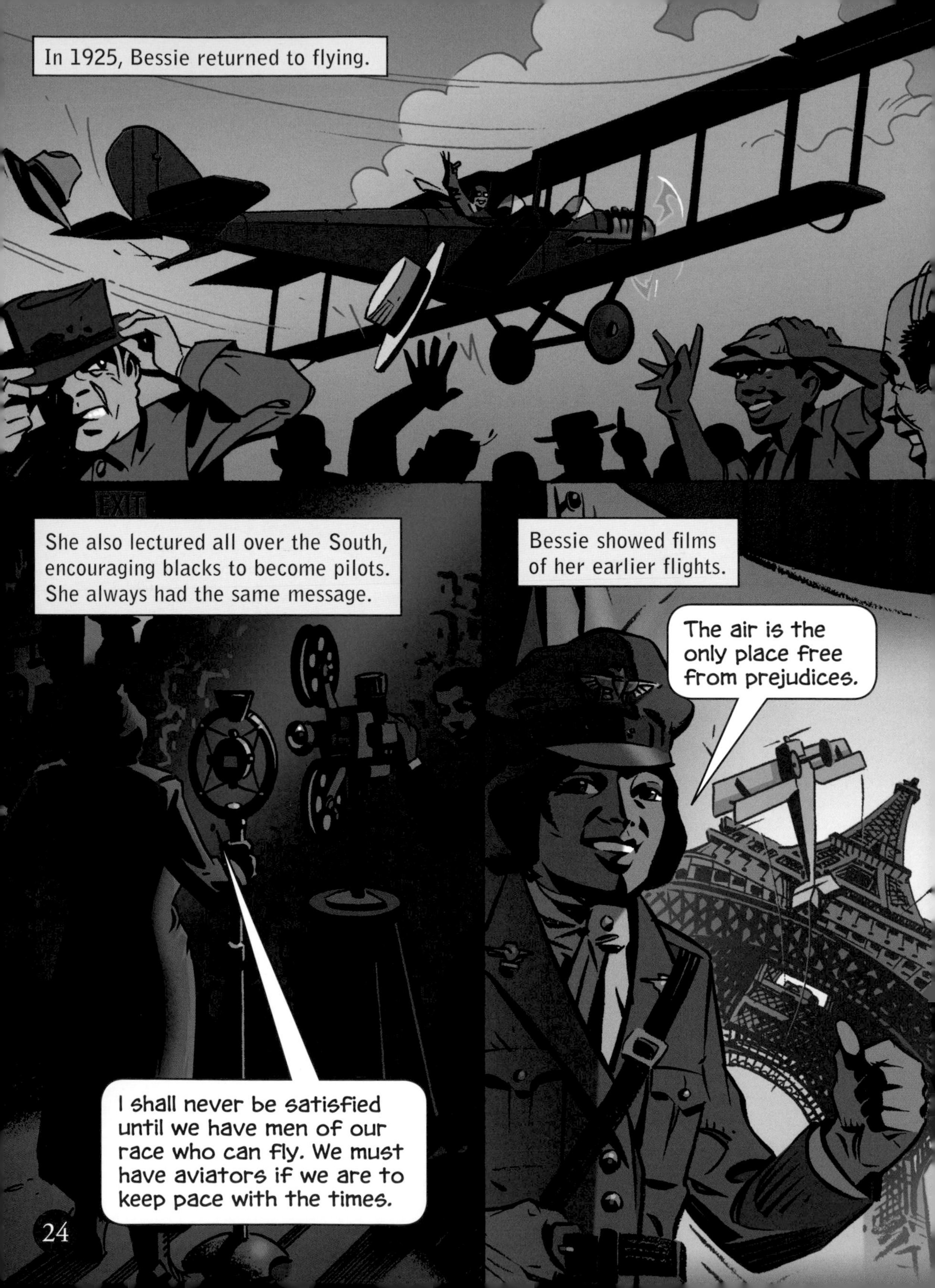
In 1925, Bessie returned to flying.
She also lectured all over the South, encouraging blacks to become pilots. She always had the same message.
I shall never be satisfied until we have men of our race who can fly. We must have aviators if we are to keep pace with the times.
Bessie showed films of her earlier flights.
The air is the only place free from prejudices.
EXIT

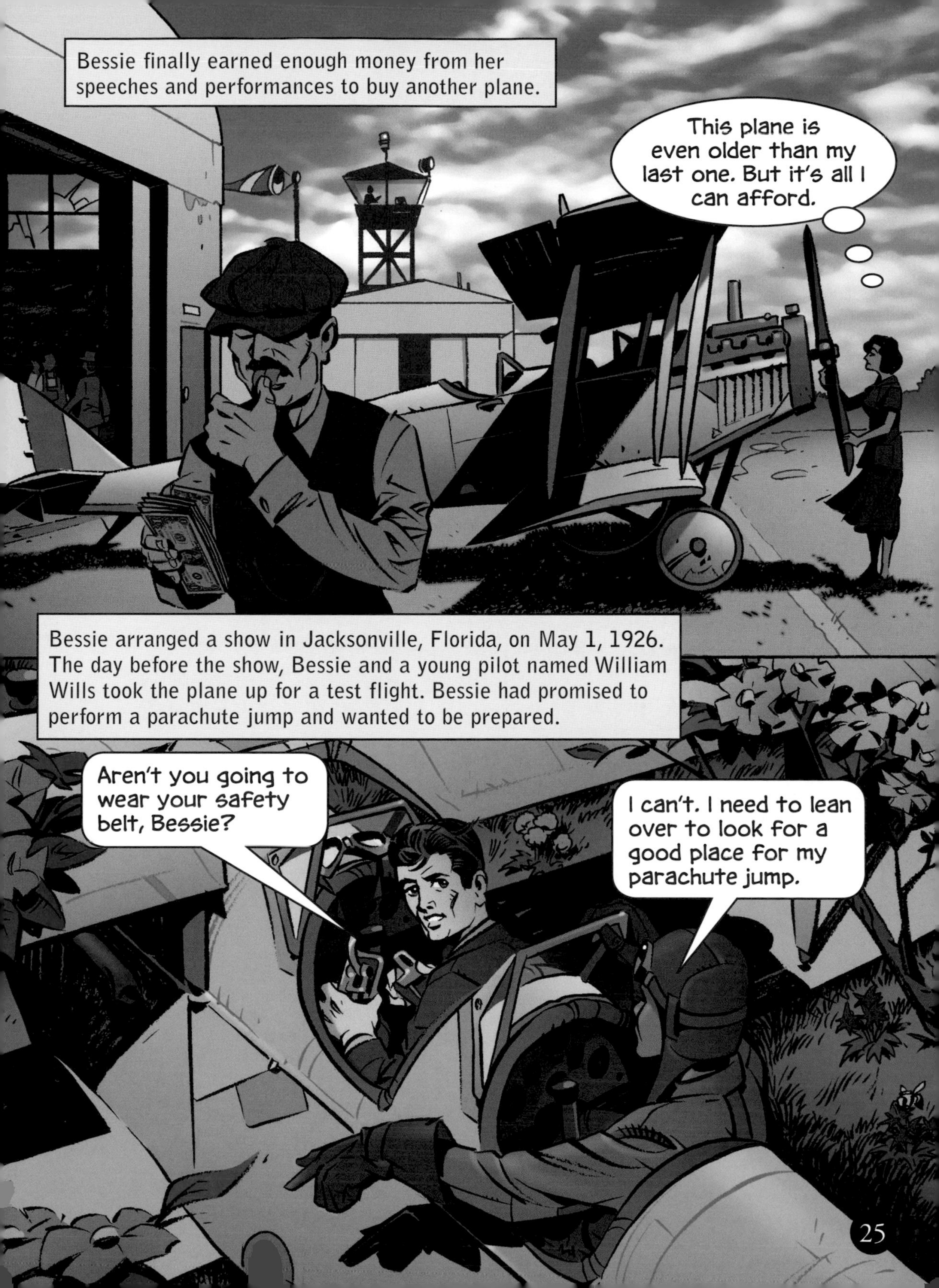
Bessie finally earned enough money from her speeches and performances to buy another plane.
This plane is even older than my last one. But it's all I can afford.
Bessie arranged a show in Jacksonville, Florida, on May 1, 1926. The day before the show, Bessie and a young pilot named William Wills took the plane up for a test flight. Bessie had promised to perform a parachute jump and wanted to be prepared.
Aren't you going to wear your safety belt, Bessie?
I can't. I need to lean over to look for a good place for my parachute jump.

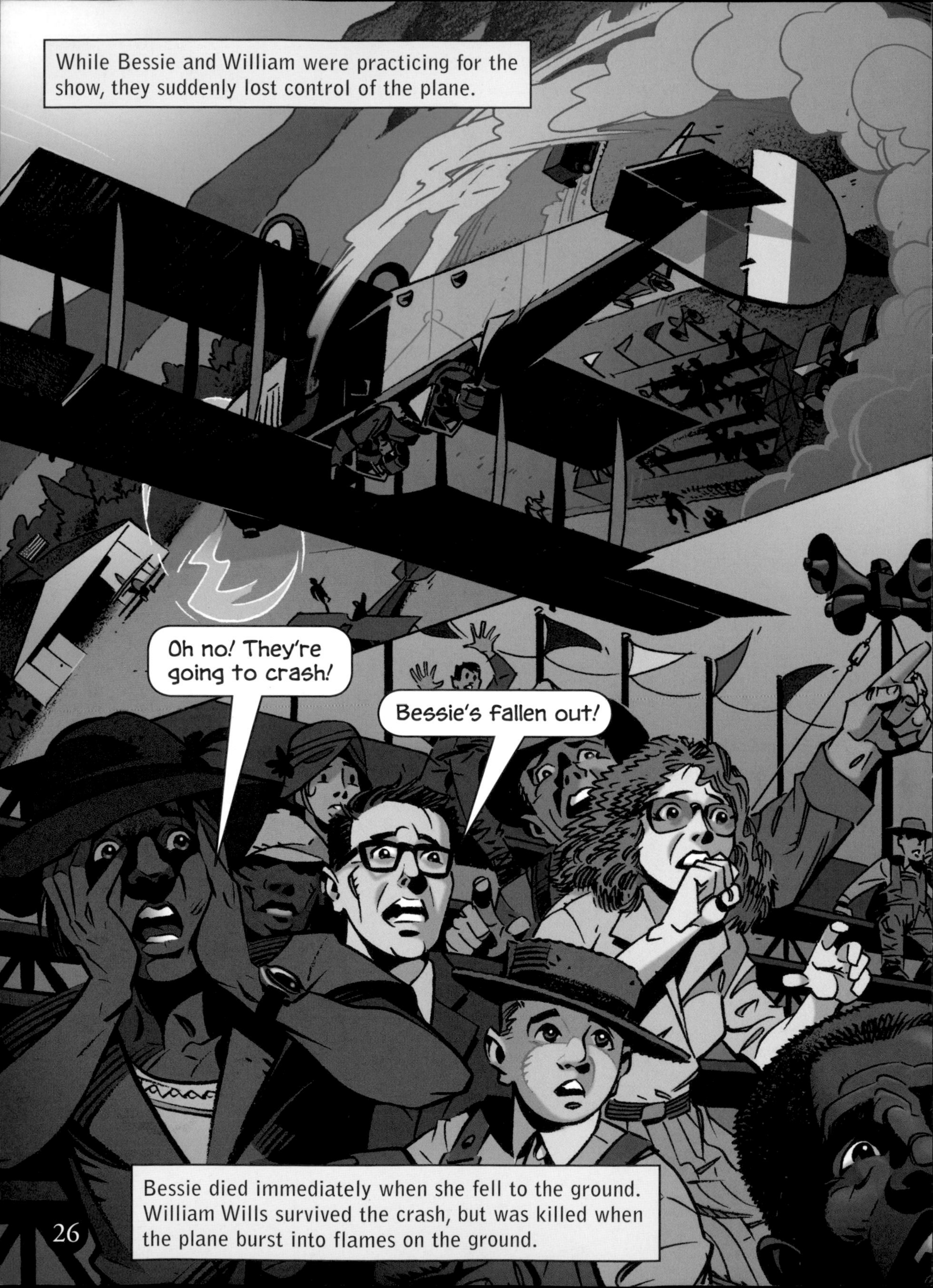
While Bessie and William were practicing for the show, they suddenly lost control of the plane.
Oh no! They're going to crash!
Bessie's fallen out!
Bessie died immediately when she fell to the ground. William Wills survived the crash, but was killed when the plane burst into flames on the ground.

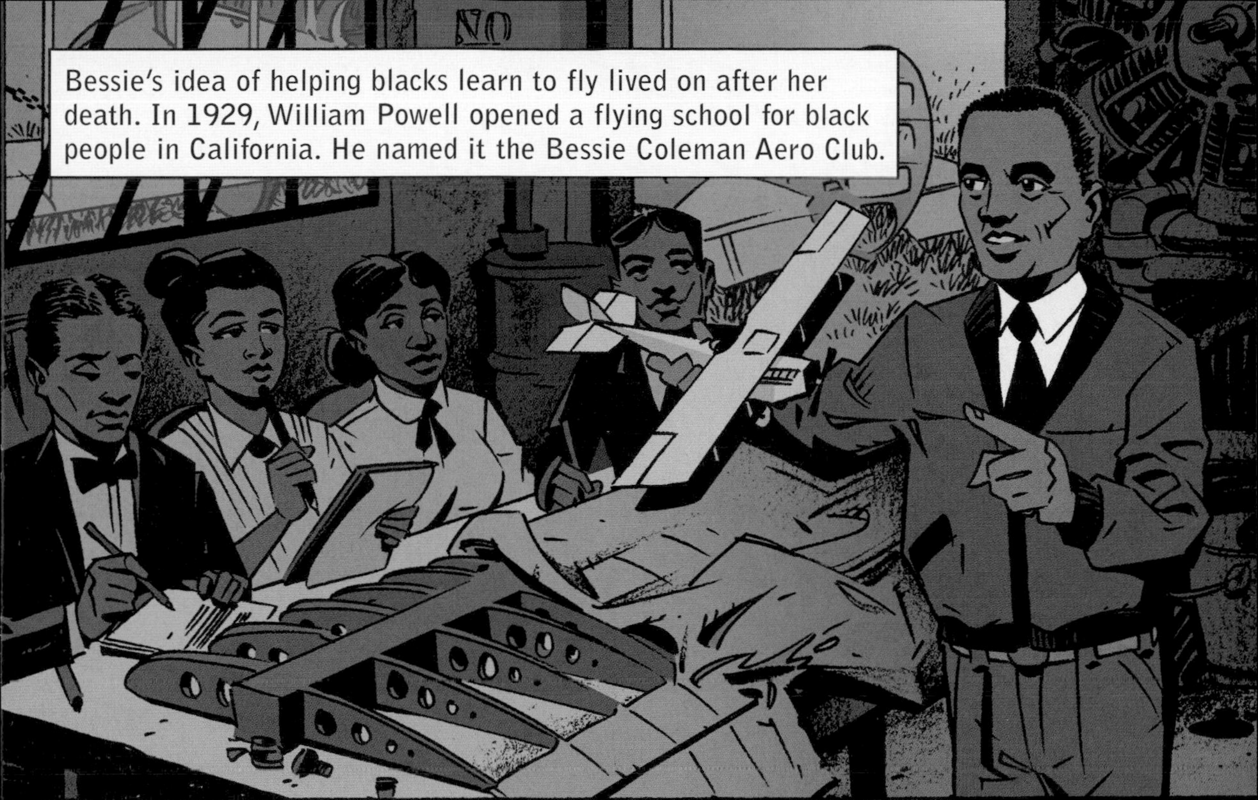
Bessie's idea of helping blacks learn to fly lived on after her death. In 1929, William Powell opened a flying school for black people in California. He named it the Bessie Coleman Aero Club.
NO

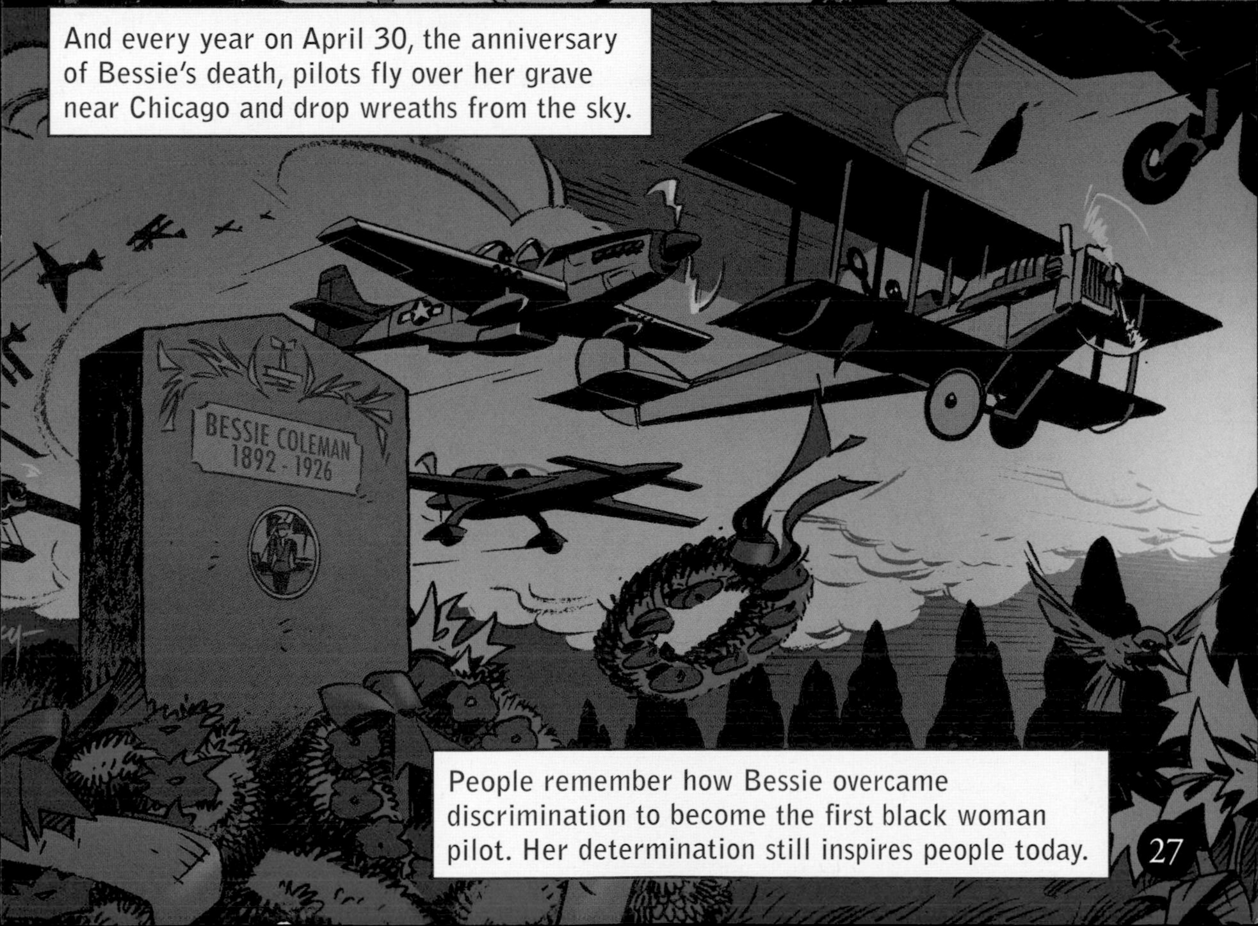
And every year on April 30, the anniversary of Bessie's death, pilots fly over her grave near Chicago and drop wreaths from the sky.
BESSIE COLEMAN
1892 - 1926
People remember how Bessie overcame discrimination to become the first black woman pilot. Her determination still inspires people today.

MORE ABOUT BESSIE COLEMAN

 Bessie was born Elizabeth Coleman on January 26, 1892. She often lied about her age. On her pilot's license, she listed her age as four years younger than she really was. She thought the younger she was, the more impressive she would seem to the public.

 Bessie's father was part Cherokee Indian. He left his family because he wanted to live in Oklahoma with the Cherokee tribe.

 Bessie's pilot's license was issued by the Fédération Aéronautique Internationale in France.

 When Bessie returned to the United States in 1921, she and her mother were invited to a performance of *Shuffle Along*, a famous all-black musical. In most theaters, black people had to sit in the balcony, but the producers of *Shuffle Along* made sure that in their theater, black people could sit in the same sections as anyone else. After the show, the performers called Bessie on stage and gave her a big silver cup engraved with the names of the cast.

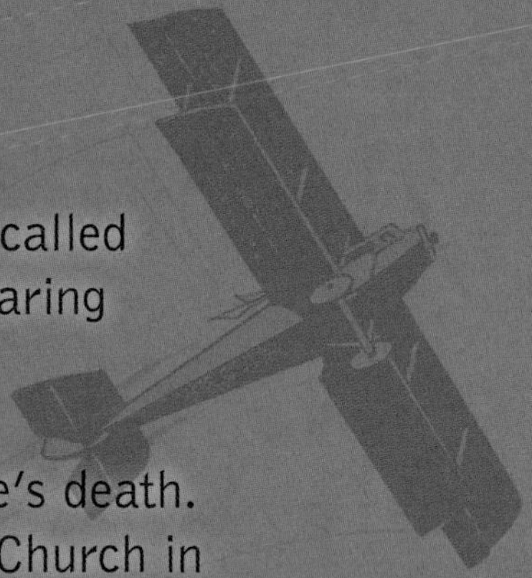

- The newspapers gave Bessie nicknames. They called her "Brave Bess," "Queen Bess," and "The Daring Manicure Girl."

- Four memorial services were held after Bessie's death. The final service was held at Pilgrim Baptist Church in Chicago. Fifteen hundred people attended and another 3,500 had to stand outside because there was no room in the church.

- After Bessie's death, people learned that a wrench had slid into the control gears and jammed them, causing the crash. Bessie's old plane did not have covered gears.

- A street near Chicago's O'Hare International Airport and a Chicago public library are named after Bessie.

- On July 14, 2000, Bessie was inducted into the Texas Aviation Hall of Fame.

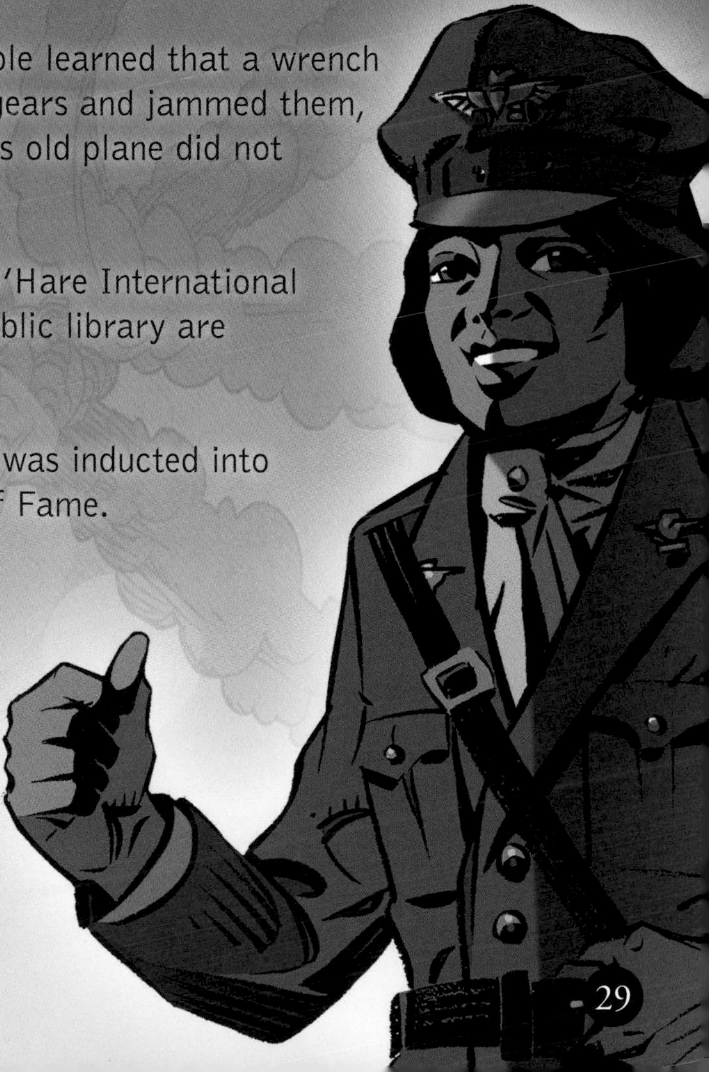

GLOSSARY

aerodynamic forces (air-oh-dye-NA-mik FORSS-ez)— something that changes the speed, direction, or motion of an object; thrust, drag, weight, and lift are four forces that let an airplane fly.

aviator (AY-ve-ay-tuhr)—a pilot of an airplane or other aircraft

aviatrix (ay-ve-AY-triks)—a female airplane pilot

manicurist (ma-nuh-KYUR-ist)—a person who cleans, trims, and polishes people's fingernails

prejudice (PREJ-uh-diss)—an opinion about others that is unfair or not based on facts

segregated (SEG-ruh-gay-ted)—separated by race

INTERNET SITES

FactHound offers a safe, fun way to find Internet sites related to this book. All of the sites on FactHound have been researched by our staff.

Here's how:
1. Visit *www.facthound.com*
2. Choose your grade level.
3. Type in this book ID **0736868518** for age-appropriate sites. You may also browse subjects by clicking on letters, or by clicking on pictures and words.
4. Click on the **Fetch It** button.

FactHound will fetch the best sites for you!

READ MORE

Borden, Louise, and Mary Kay Kroeger. *Fly High! The Story of Bessie Coleman.* New York: Margaret K. McElderry Books, 2001.

Grimes, Nikki. *Talkin' about Bessie: The Story of Elizabeth Coleman.* New York: Orchard Books, 2002.

Hart, Philip S. *Up in the Air: the Story of Bessie Coleman.* Minneapolis: Carolrhoda Books, 1996.

McLoone, Margo. *Women Explorers of the Air.* Capstone Short Biographies. Capstone Books: Mankato, Minn., 2000.

BIBLIOGRAPHY

"Aviatrix Must Sign Away Life to Learn Trade." *Chicago Defender.* October 8, 1921.

Boase, Wendy. *The Sky's The Limit: Women Pioneers in Aviation.* New York: Macmillan, 1979.

Freydberg, Elizabeth Amelia Hadley. *Bessie Coleman: The Brownskin Lady Bird.* Studies in African American History and Culture. New York: Garland Publishing, 1994.

Moolman, Valerie. *Women Aloft.* The Epic of Flight. Alexandria, Va.: Time-Life Books, 1981.

Rich, Doris L. *Queen Bess: Daredevil Aviator.* Washington, D.C.: Smithsonian Institution Press, 1993.

INDEX

Abbott, Robert, 11, 15, 21
Aviation School of the
    Caudron Brothers, 16

Bessie Coleman Aero Club,
    27
Bullard, Eugene, 12

Chicago Defender
    (newspaper), 8, 11, 12, 15,
    21
Coleman, Bessie
    birth of, 28
    death of, 26–27, 29
    in flight school, 16–18
    and flying accidents, 22,
        26
    jobs of, 5, 7, 8, 11, 20
    and pilot's license, 18, 28
    and school, 4, 5, 6
    as stunt pilot, 21–22,
        24–25

Coleman, Georgia (sister), 12
Coleman, John (brother), 8,
    11, 12, 13
Coleman, Susan (mother), 4,
    5, 9, 12
Coleman, Walter (brother), 8,
    9, 11, 12, 20
Colored Agriculture and
    Normal University, 6

discrimination, 7, 14, 20, 27

Quimby, Harriet, 7, 8

segregation, 6, 10

Uncle Tom's Cabin, 4

Wills, William, 25
World War I, 12